GOVERNOR'S RESIDENCE
Cookbook

GOVERNOR'S RESIDENCE
Cookbook

June McCarthy
Executive Chef for the Governor's Residence

Introduction by
Hope Taft, First Lady of Ohio

ORANGE FRAZER *PRESS*
Wilmington, Ohio

ISBN 1-933197-15-3
Copyright 2006 Governor's Residence Foundation

Additional copies of the Governor's Residence Cookbook
may be ordered directly from:

Orange Frazer Press
P.O. Box 214
Wilmington, OH 45177

Telephone 1.800.852.9332 for price and shipping information.
Website: www.orangefrazer.com

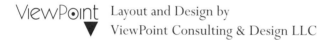 Layout and Design by
ViewPoint Consulting & Design LLC

Library of Congress Control Number: 2006923744

Dedication

Like a wedding cake, each governor's family has added a layer of history to the Ohio Governor's Residence. It has been called the Executive Mansion, the Governor's Mansion, and the Governor's Residence. It has been a welcoming home to children, dogs, cats, fish, ducks and alligators. It has hosted some of the leading citizens of the nation. It has been the site for important decisions in the history of Ohio.

Living in the Governor's Residence is a very special time in the life of a family. Melding family traditions and public duties takes thoughtful planning. This huge task is made possible by the wonderful staff whose job it is to keep the house running smoothly so home life does not distract from the public life and duties of the governor and first lady. This book is dedicated to all the fine men and women who have so ably and lovingly filled this role.

ACKNOWLEDGEMENTS

Getting any book from the idea stage into the hands of the reader is an enormous undertaking. This historical cookbook is no exception.

The idea was conceived by June McCarthy, the part-time Residence Chef who decided that when she stopped teaching Family and Consumer Science at Newark High School, she would have a lot of time on her hands. She has the perfect background and connections for such an undertaking. June's Bachelor of Science degree in Home Economics Education led her to a 30-year teaching career where she did her best to inspire young people to eat healthy and present their cooking with a creative flair. She worked with Betty Rosbottom at La Belle Pomme, a popular Columbus cooking school, where she learned the art and skill of cooking for large crowds. June was hired by the Voinovich Administration as the chef for the Governor's Residence and has been responsible for most of the food served here since 1995. She organized the first two National Governors' Association conferences for chefs of governors' residences. June had the opportunity to help prepare a dinner in honor of the Governors of the States and Territories and a luncheon for the Governors' spouses hosted by First Lady Laura Bush at the White House in February 2006.

She was a friend of Frannie Packard, the chef during the Celeste Administration, so had access to the favorite recipes of four First Families. She has selected the best of the best, tested them again and again, and added notes to help you do things the easy way to keep your cooking time close to 30 minutes. The Tafts enjoyed tasting each one. We all are indebted to Betty O'Neill, Brad Bloomer, Sue Moore, Ellen Gilligan, Dagmar Celeste, Janet Voinovich, and Nancy Hollister for graciously sharing their favorite family recipes and stories.

June has also been active in the Ohio Department of Agriculture's Ohio Proud program, is familiar with many of their products and knows where to find the best ingredients in the state. We would like to thank Director Fred Daily and the marketing department for their help and Ohio Proud members Graeter's, Marzetti's, Miceli's Dairy Products, Robert Rothschild Farm, and Smucker's for helping to underwrite this cookbook.

June's son and daughter-in-law, Keary and Lori McCarthy, have their own business, Viewpoint Consulting and Design LLC, a public relations and design firm. Thankfully, they took on the responsibility for layout and design. Lori spent hours formatting the book so its historical aspects would add to your cooking pleasure.

Since the book is more than a cookbook, we would like to thank Mary Alice Mairose, Curator for the Governor's Residence Foundation, for the historical research and the Ohio Historical Society and Kent State University for the photographs included in the book.

No book can go to press without good proofreading. We would like to thank Lee Ann Parsons, school librarian and docent at the Residence, for her editing and June's sister-in-law, Tara Reeder, a great cook and critical taster, for her comments on the ease of understanding the recipes. We wanted to make sure your results are as good as those served at the Residence!

This book would not have happened without the leadership and support of Marcie Seidel, Chief of Staff to the First Lady, and Julie Stone, Residence Manager, who volunteered many hours of help. Marcy Hawley at Orange Frazer Press came to our rescue at a critical point just before publication. Her knowledge and expertise makes this book look wonderful, open flat, and stay together, which are three things very important to cooks!

We hope you enjoy all the hard work by this volunteer team of people who want to share a 'taste of life' in the Ohio Governor's Residence. The proceeds of their efforts and your generosity go to the Governor's Residence Foundation, a nonpartisan, non-profit organization dedicated to preserving, sustaining and enhancing the Ohio Governor's Residence and Heritage Garden so it can continue to educate and inspire people about the many facets of our state's history.

Hope Taft

GOVERNORS WHO HAVE LIVED AT THE RESIDENCE	
Bob and Hope Taft	1999–2007
Nancy and Jeff Hollister	Dec. 31, 1998–Jan. 11, 1999
George V. and Janet Voinovich	1991–1998
Richard F. and Dagmar Celeste	1983–1991
John J. and Katie Gilligan	1971–1975
James A. and Helen Rhodes	1963–1971 and 1975–1983
Michael V. and Myrtle DiSalle	1959–1963
C. William and Betty O'Neill	1957–1959

TABLE OF CONTENTS

INTRODUCTION

by Mrs. Hope Taft, First Lady of Ohio

The residence, at 358 North Parkview Avenue in Bexley, was designed in 1925 for entertaining. When Governor O'Neill and his family made it their home in 1957, entertaining took on a new meaning. The day she moved in, Mrs. O'Neill showed off the newly acquired Executive Residence to hundreds of female reporters. We still have some of the cup and saucer plates used to make her many large teas possible. We also have many delightful stories about happenings at the Residence.

The O'Neills' young children had lots of pets. They had hamsters that would invariably escape and start running around just as company arrived. Once the cat appeared at an inappropriate moment and scared a reporter so badly she climbed onto the top of the back of the davenport. The most unusual pet that ever lived at the Residence was a baby alligator that Congressman Chalmers Wylie brought back from Florida for the children. It lived for a short while in an upstairs bathtub.

Governor DiSalle was one of seven children. When all the relatives gathered for holiday meals, he had to set up two rows of long tables in the largest room in the house to accommodate them all. When his daughter, Barbara, was married, the long receiving line wound its way through the Residence and out the back door to the garden where the punch bowl was located. The line was so long, the bride finally kicked her shoes off and that was the photo the papers decided to print.

Mrs. Rhodes brought her own tea service with her when they moved into the Governor's Residence for all the entertaining she knew she would do. It complemented the tea service known as the McKinley silver. In fact, we still use the Ohio Executive Mansion tea napkins and match books that were printed during the Rhodes Administration. One of her granddaughters caused a commotion at one of these teas when she hid under the dining room table for so long her parents thought she had run away! Bob Hope, Lionel Hampton, Pat Boone and Art Linkletter came to visit here when they performed at the state fair.

Mrs. Gilligan's family tells the story of her dropping the vegetable dish the night she learned, while cooking, that her eldest daughter was engaged. It is said she scooped the French fried eggplant up from the floor, put it on a fancy platter and presented it with great flair in the dining room. The wedding reception that soon followed was the last party the Gilligans had at the Residence. Kathleen and Gary Sebelius' wedding was the fourth of many wedding receptions held here for children of governors, although Kathleen, the current Governor of Kansas, is the first to become a governor in her own right. When the Gilligans entertained the Ohio General Assembly in three back-to-back dinner parties, they discovered that many had never been to the Residence before. The silver from the decommissioned battleship USS Ohio was returned to Ohio at the request of Governor Gilligan.

As a new first lady, Mrs. Celeste asked Mrs. Rhodes for advice and was told, "Never stand in a receiving line in your own home." Mrs. Celeste took this advice to heart. She and Governor Celeste entertained a lot. Peter, Paul, and Mary, Jesse Jackson and Roselyn Carter are some of the more famous guests during their time. There is one story of a dinner party with actress Lily Tomlin as the honored guest. She performed a trick by balancing a spoon on her nose. She convinced the Governor to try this and managed to run the spoon over the candle flame before each of his attempts. His nose ended up smudged with black soot! A favorite time for the family was Sunday morning when Governor Celeste made the pancakes. So many people wanted souvenirs of their visit, the Celestes had paper napkins printed with "Ohio Governor's Residence" on them. This supply finally ran out in 2005.

Mrs. Voinovich entertained Barbara Bush at tea during Ameriflora 1992. Governor Voinovich welcomed the Rev. Billy Graham to the Residence, as well as the five astronauts who were on the Ohio shuttle. Four were from Ohio and the fifth was made an honorary citizen of the state the night before they helped the Governor open the Ohio State Fair. Governor and Mrs. Voinovich returned a Jacobean look to the Residence furniture and created a commission to oversee the public areas. Their oldest son held his wedding reception here.

Although Nancy Hollister was governor for only eleven days, she and her extended family moved in and experienced life in the Residence to the fullest. She nursed a sick husband and had to deal with a state snow emergency and a hostage situation. She also strategically placed buckets in the Great Room to catch water leaks, and hosted a festive New Year's Eve party for her extended family. During the final farewell staff party, they broke the tension by counting the bathrooms in the Residence, all 12 of them!

We have tried to carry on the entertaining traditions at the Governor's Residence. Governor George W. Bush, actor Henry Winkler, Ohio singing stars Kathleen Battle and Sylvia McNair, and Ohio author Ann Hagedorn have shared meals with us. Receptions and barbeques in the new Heritage Garden, a botanical garden of native plants representing all areas of Ohio, have become a frequent occurrence.

Docent-led tours make the governor's home a welcoming place for Ohio citizens to visit and learn about the state's artistic, industrial, political and horticultural contributions to the world. The Heritage Garden, based on the state's geology, uniquely ties this Tudor house to its Ohio roots.

We hope you enjoy this Governor's Residence Cookbook that combines the favorite recipes of the First Families who have lived here and some of the history they have made. It is one more way we can educate Ohio citizens about the people's home and encourage them to explore a culinary world filled with food that not only is healthy and delicious to eat but also gives them a taste of life in the Governor's Residence. This cookbook gives you a "peek into the lives of the governors that have served our great state and the great food they have served."

Enjoy!

Hope Taft
First Lady of Ohio
1999–2007

PREFACE

by June McCarthy, Executive Chef for the Governor's Residence

One memorable day in 1995 I received a phone call from my friend, Frannie Packard. She exclaimed, "I'm going to Italy and you're going to take my job." This wasn't just any job; this was a major career advancement. You see, Frannie was the Governor's Residence Executive Chef. My first reaction was disbelief and shock. However, her predictions came to fruition later that year when, after an exciting but nerve-racking trial period, I was indeed offered the position. This began a bountiful career that to this day has transcended my personal and professional expectations. It has been my honor and delight to serve three of Ohio's First Families.

Using restaurant terms, Mrs. Taft has given you history about the "front of the house." I would like to give you some history of the "back of the house." The earliest kitchen assistants at the Governor's Residence were not specifically appointed or trained. In fact, they were inmates from the old Ohio Penitentiary who had reached "trustee" status.

The Celeste Administration hired the first titled chef, Nonni Casino. Also during the Celeste term, Rodney Helser was hired as the Major Domo. His responsibilities entailed all aspects of entertaining at the Residence. Rodney is remarkably talented. He can set and adorn a table for a State Dinner Party like no one else. He is an invaluable person with whom to brainstorm ideas. Rodney served in that position through the Celeste Term. He is still a good friend of the Residence and shares his talents when asked. John Crawford served as Residence Chef after Nonni and before Frannie Packard was hired in 1987. I have not had the pleasure of meeting John or Nonni, but everything I have heard has been very complimentary. Frannie, who is a personal friend, is a very imaginative and gifted chef.

As a chef and mother of a precious family, the kitchen has always been the heart of my home, and a place that is rich in both history and traditions. It is where family and friends gather, conversations flourish and people reconnect. In short, it is where the body is nourished and the spirit is restored. It is this simple philosophy that consistently guides my actions in the Residence kitchen whether it is leaving an easy breakfast muffin batter (see page 99) for a winter's Cabinet breakfast or staying late to provide a much-deserved hot meal for the Governor. If I can provide this sustenance to the First Families I have grown to love, then I am confident I have done my best.

One of my greatest rewards has been to witness the positive transformations that occur at the end of a tiring day when families gather around their favorite meal. Stress and fatigue are replaced by tranquility, vitality, and contentment. I have been privileged to be part of this process at the Governor's table and I hold these years close to my heart. It is with great joy that I share the recipes that have been favorites of our Ohio First Families. To use a culinary metaphor, these recipes "rose like the cream to the top." It has also been a professional thrill to be part of Ohio history, albeit small but significant.

"The most indispensable ingredient of all good home cooking: love for those you are cooking for."

—— Sophia Loren, 1963

June McCarthy

FIRST COURSES & APPETIZERS

C. WILLIAM O'NEILL

GOVERNOR OF OHIO
1957–1959

In 1938, at the age of 22, C. William O'Neill was elected to The Ohio House of Representatives as a representative from Marietta. He eventually served as Speaker of the House and Minority Leader. His legislative duties were interrupted from 1943 to 1946 while he served with General Patton's Third Army. He was Attorney General for three terms before serving as Governor from 1957 through 1959. Governor O'Neill then served on the Ohio Supreme Court from 1960 until his death in 1978 and was Chief Justice for the last eight years. He had the distinction of serving in all three branches of Ohio government.

Photo courtesy of the Ohio Historical Society SC 3653

Photo courtesy of the Ohio Historical Society SC 3653

Governor C. William O'Neill and his family were the first to reside in the Residence. First Lady Betty O'Neill gave many Ohioans the opportunity to visit the Residence by hosting many teas and tours. The Today Show, hosted by Dave Garroway, did a feature on education that was broadcast from the Residence during the O'Neill Administration.

BETTY O'NEILL'S SHRIMP AU GRATIN

2 tablespoons unsalted butter

2 tablespoons Pillsbury Unbleached All-Purpose Flour

1 cup milk

½ teaspoon salt

Freshly ground pepper to taste

1 (10 ounce) can Cheddar cheese soup

1 pound shrimp, shelled, deveined and cooked

1 cup Swiss or Cheddar cheese, shredded

* * * * * *

Fresh Italian parsley, chopped

CHEF'S NOTE

I prefer Italian parsley over curley parsley because the flavor is more robust.

1. Preheat oven to 400 degrees. Generously butter 8 (4 ounce) ramekins.

2. In a large heavy skillet over medium heat, melt butter. Stir in the flour, and cook for about a minute. Gradually whisk in the milk, salt, and pepper. Cook, stirring constantly, until sauce bubbles and thickens. While stirring, add soup and shrimp; bring again to a low boil. Divide mixture among the ramekins; top each with cheese.

3. Bake in preheated oven for 10–15 minutes or until gratin is bubbly and cheese has browned. Serve immediately. Garnish with parsley.

Serves: 8

Photo courtesy of the Ohio Historical Society P95

Ruth Lyons, an early television personality from Cincinnati complimented Mrs. O'Neill at one of her many teas on starting a new trend…serving tea in cups with no saucers. Mrs. O'Neill had to admit she wasn't intentionally starting a trend. The Residence simply didn't have enough saucers for such a large crowd. After repeating the story the next day on her show, saucers began arriving at the Residence by the dozens.

AVOCADO LOBSTER

2–3 lobster tails

* * * * * *

1 cup sweet corn, cooked, cut off husk, cooled

4 Roma tomatoes, chopped and seeded

2 tablespoons shallots, minced

2 tablespoons fresh cilantro, chopped

2 teaspoons fresh lemon juice

Salt and freshly ground pepper to taste

* * * * * *

¼ cup honey

2 tablespoons spicy mustard

2 teaspoons fresh lemon juice

1 teaspoon sesame oil

2 teaspoons olive oil

* * * * * *

3 ripe avocados, peeled, cut in half, tossed with lemon juice

Fresh lemon juice

Melted butter

1. Cook lobster in boiling salted water for 8 minutes. Stop cooking by shocking the lobster in ice water. Drain and chill. Remove meat from shells, and coarsely chop. Kitchen scissors are most helpful for this task. Reserve.

2. For the salsa, combine the corn, tomatoes, shallots, cilantro, lemon juice, salt, and pepper. Reserve.

3. For the sauce, whisk together the honey, mustard, lemon juice, sesame oil, and olive oil. Pour into a squirt bottle and reserve.

4. To assemble, place each avocado cut side down and make ¼" slices lengthwise, keeping avocado intact. Carefully slide the slices in a straight line and then into a circle; place on a serving plate (if avocados are not quite ripe and placing them in a circle is difficult, simply fan out slices on serving plate and top with lobster). Fill the avocado with lobster meat. Drizzle with lemon juice and melted butter. Top with salsa and drizzle with a little bit of sauce. Garnish the plate and lobster with chopped cilantro. Drizzle the plate with the sauce.

Serves: 6

CHEF'S NOTE

This is an impressive and tasty first course. I served this at a State Dinner Party. Ten Governors were in town for a conference with Governor George Voinovich. They all clapped at the end of the meal. I think it's safe to assume that they all loved it.

SOUFFLÉ WITH BRIE AND APRICOTS

6 tablespoons unsalted butter, softened

8 slices good quality white sandwich bread, crusts removed

2 cups milk

¾ teaspoon salt

Dash Tabasco

4 eggs

1¼ pound Brie, rind removed

* * * * * *

GARNISH

½ cup dried apricots, chopped

2 tablespoons fresh parsley, chopped

1. Preheat the oven to 350 degrees. Butter a 2-quart casserole dish.

2. Soak the apricots in 1 cup of boiling water for about 30 minutes. This will make a nice moist garnish for the Brie. Reserve.

3. Butter one side of each slice of bread and cut in half to make 2 triangles. Whisk together the milk, salt, Tobasco, and eggs. Coarsely shred the Brie (can also use a food processor with the medium shred disc).

4. Arrange half the bread, buttered side up, on the bottom of the dish. Sprinkle evenly with half the Brie and then repeat using all the bread and the Brie. Pour the egg mixture over the bread. Let stand at room temperature for least 15 minutes or can be made ahead.

5. Bake for 25–30 minutes or until bubbling and golden. Let rest for at least 15 minutes.

6. When ready to serve, garnish with apricots and parsley.

Serves: 6–8 (First course servings)

CHEF'S NOTE

If you partially freeze the Brie, it will be easier to shred.

Serve the Brie as a continental dessert. Nestle some beautiful fresh fruit next to it.

LAYERED LEMON POTATO AND CILANTRO CHICKEN

8 medium potatoes, peeled
4–6 tablespoons fresh lemon juice
Salt and freshly ground pepper to taste
4 chicken breasts, skinned and boned
4 scallions, minced
1 stalk celery, minced
½ cup fresh cilantro, chopped
½ cup green pepper, minced
Juice of one lemon
Mayonnaise

* * * * * *

¼ cup mayonnaise
Whole cilantro leaves

1. Cook potatoes in salted water over medium-high heat until tender. Drain; put potatoes through a potato ricer. Add enough lemon juice to make a moist mashed potato. Season with salt and pepper.

2. In a heavy saucepan, combine the chicken breasts with enough salted cold water to cover them by 1". Bring the water to a simmer. Poach chicken at barely a simmer for about 15 minutes or until there is no pink inside the chicken. Remove the chicken from the liquid and allow to cool.

3. Shred and chop chicken. Place in a mixing bowl with the scallions, celery, cilantro, and green pepper. Sprinkle with lemon juice, fold in enough mayonnaise to make a moist chicken salad consistency. Season with salt and pepper.

4. Spray a round (10"–12") shallow casserole dish with Crisco Non-Stick Spray. Line the dish with plastic wrap. Spread half the potato mixture on the bottom of the dish. Top with the chicken salad, smoothly and evenly. Spread the remaining lemon potatoes over the chicken salad. Press firmly into the dish. Chill for several hours.

5. To serve, invert onto serving platter. Remove the plastic wrap. Spread a thin layer of mayonnaise over and around the layered potatoes and chicken. Garnish decoratively with cilantro leaves.

CHEF'S NOTE

A small slice served with a mesclun salad is a very nice first course. A larger piece served with a salad is a wonderful luncheon dish.

A good quality canned whole chicken can be substituted for the poached chicken.

Serves: 16

CRAB CAKES WITH SPICY LEMON REMOULADE

CRAB CAKES

1 egg

2 tablespoons light mayonnaise

4 teaspoons Dijon mustard

1½ tablespoons fresh lemon juice

1 pound best quality crabmeat (claw or chunk), drained and patted dry

¼ cup scallions, minced

2 tablespoons fresh parsley, chopped

Zest from one lemon

1 cup fresh breadcrumbs, divided

½ tablespoon Old Bay Seafood seasoning

¼ teaspoon salt

Dash cayenne pepper

1 tablespoon each butter and olive oil

SPICY LEMON REMOULADE SAUCE

2 sticks unsalted butter

2 egg yolks

1 shallot, chopped

2 tablespoons Dijon mustard

3 tablespoons fresh lemon juice

1 teaspoon lemon zest

2 tablespoons cornichons*, coarsely chopped

2 tablespoons Crosse & Blackwell Capers

1 tablespoon fresh tarragon, chopped

1 tablespoon fresh parsley, chopped

½ teaspoon freshly ground pepper

¼ teaspoon salt

Dash Tabasco sauce

1. For the crab cakes, combine the egg, mayonnaise, mustard, and lemon juice in a large bowl. Add the crabmeat, scallions, parsley, lemon zest, ¾ cup breadcrumbs, salt, pepper, and bay seasonings. Mix well. Shape into 1½" flat cakes. Dust outside of each cake with remaining breadcrumbs. Place crab cakes on a baking sheet; cover loosely with plastic wrap and refrigerate.

2. Heat butter and oil in a large heavy skillet over medium heat. When hot, add cakes and cook each side until nicely browned. Repeat until all cakes are cooked; use extra oil and butter if needed. Keep crab cakes warm on a paper towel lined baking sheet in a warm oven.

3. For the sauce: Melt the butter in a small, heavy saucepan over medium heat until bubbling; keep hot. Place egg yolks, shallots, mustard, lemon juice, and zest in the bowl of a food processor fitted with the steel blade. Process to combine. With the machine running, pour the hot butter in a fine stream through the feed tube. Remove the sauce to a warm bowl and stir in the cornichons, capers, herbs, salt, pepper and hot sauce to taste. Keep warm.

CHEF'S NOTE

Cornichons are small pickled gherkin cucumbers found in gourmet food shops. They can easily be substituted with small dill pickles.

This Remoulade sauce cannot be rewarmed. To keep warm, place pan in a water bath.

Serves: 1–2 dozen

"MELT IN YOUR MOUTH" NIBBLERS

¾ cup flour

¼ teaspoon celery salt

¼ teaspoon salt

Freshly ground pepper to taste

6 tablespoons unsalted butter, cubed and chilled

⅔ cup cheddar cheese, grated

2 tablespoons Miceli's Grated Parmesan Cheese

1 egg yolk

* * * * * *

1 egg, beaten

Miceli's Grated Parmesan Cheese

Poppy seeds

Sesame seeds

1. Preheat oven to 375 degrees. Line sheet pans with parchment paper.

2. Mix together the flour, celery salt, salt, and freshly ground pepper in a medium bowl. Add butter. With a pastry blender, cut in the butter until a lot of the flour has been absorbed. Add both cheeses and continue cutting in until the mixture is blended and coming together in rough clumps. Add the egg yolk and bring the mixture together; form a ball. Wrap loosely in plastic wrap and flatten. Chill.

3. Roll dough out on lightly floured surface to ¼" thickness. Cut in triangles to desired size. Brush with egg wash; sprinkle with your choice of toppings. Transfer to baking sheets. Chill before baking.

4. Bake in preheated oven for 10 minutes or until golden.

Yield: 5 dozen

CHEF'S NOTE

Governor and Mrs. Taft hosted a National Governors' Association Meeting at the Residence. Guests included spouses' assistants, Residence Managers, and Residence Chefs. They all loved this "nibbler"—the chefs even requested the recipe.

These "nibblers" freeze very well.

MARINATED OLIVES AND FETA CHEESE

1 cup Kalamata olives or other brine-cured black olives
1 cup green olives
¾ cup extra-virgin olive oil, divided
6 tablespoons fresh lemon juice, divided
4 garlic cloves, thinly sliced
2 tablespoons fresh Italian parsley, chopped
2 teaspoons lemon zest
1 teaspoon dried oregano, divided
⅛ teaspoon dried crushed red pepper
½ teaspoon black pepper
10 ounces feta cheese cut into ½" cubes

1. Mix both olives, ½ cup olive oil, 3 tablespoons lemon juice, garlic, parsley, lemon zest, ½ teaspoon oregano, and red pepper in a resealable plastic bag. Marinate for a couple of hours.

2. In a large bowl, carefully combine the feta, remaining olive oil, lemon juice, and oregano. Season with black pepper.

3. With a slotted spoon, place the olives in the center of a serving platter. Arrange the feta cheese mixture around the olives. Garnish with fresh parsley.

Serves: 10

CHEF'S NOTE

These herbed olives are a nice addition to a crudités (vegetable) platter for an hors d'oeuvre party.

BRIE WITH CRANBERRY RASPBERRY CHUTNEY

½ cup water

2 cups sugar

1 (12 ounce) package of fresh cranberries

2 cups raspberries

¼ cup cider vinegar

2 tablespoons brown sugar

1 teaspoon ground ginger

1 cup walnuts, toasted and chopped

* * * * * *

1 pound round of Brie

* * * * * *

Toasted French bread slices

1. Place the sugar and water in a large heavy saucepan and bring to a boil. Add all the ingredients except the walnuts. Bring to medium-high and boil until the mixture is slightly thick, about 10 minutes. Remember the mixture will continue to thicken as it cools. Add the walnuts and remove from the heat.

2. Preheat oven to 350 degrees.

3. Cover baking sheet with aluminum foil and spray with Crisco Non-Stick Spray. Remove Brie from its packaging and place on the baking sheet. Bake in preheated oven until the Brie just begins to soften, about 10–15 minutes.

4. Using the foil, remove the Brie to a serving platter. Top with the chutney. Serve with French bread slices.

Serves: 16

CHEF'S NOTE

This recipe comes from a former Residence Chef and my very talented friend, Frannie Packard. Great recipes can live from one administration to the next!

* * * * * *

It is important to use a large saucepan; when the cranberries boil, they foam and pop and need lots of room.

CHICKPEAS AND ROSEMARY WITH PITA CHIPS

4 pita bread

Olive oil

* * * * * *

½ tablespoon olive oil

1 cup scallions, chopped

2 (15½ ounce) cans chickpeas, rinsed and drained

2 teaspoons fresh rosemary, chopped

½ teaspoon salt

2 tablespoons fresh lemon juice

¼ cup vegetable stock

1. Preheat oven to 350 degrees.

2. Spilt each pita; brush lightly with olive oil. Cut each pita half in 8 equal pieces. Place on baking sheet in a single layer. Bake until golden brown, about 8–10 minutes

3. Heat oil in large heavy skillet over medium heat; add scallions and sauté until tender. Add chickpeas and sauté about a minute. Remove mixture to the bowl of a food processor or blender. Add the rosemary, salt, lemon juice, and vegetable stock; process until smooth. Place in a decorative serving bowl; garnish with rosemary sprig. Serve with pita chips.

Yields: 1½ cups

CHEF'S NOTE

If you want quick and easy, pipe a rosette of the chick pea mixture onto Wheat Thins. If you want really yummy, pipe onto "Melt In Your Mouth Nibblers" (page 8).

ROASTED RED PEPPER, ONION AND MOZZARELLA TARTS

2 packages Athens Mini Fillo Shells
8 ounces fresh Mozzarella cut in ½" cubes
1 cup Robert Rothschild Roasted Red Pepper and Onion Relish

1. Preheat oven to 375 degrees.

2. Place a fillo tart in each cup of a 24 capacity mini muffin tin or 2 (12 cup) capacity tins. Place a cube of mozzarella in each cup. Bake in preheated oven for 8–10 minutes or until cheese has melted.

3. Top each tart with ½ teaspoon roasted red pepper and onion relish. Serve warm.

Serves: 12–15

CHEF'S NOTE

For a very attractive display on your serving platter, top every other tart with pesto instead of the relish. Your guests will devour them.

Photo courtesy of the Ohio Historical Society SC 512

The Governor's Residence dining room during the O'Neill Administration.

GRILLED SALMON RIBBONS WITH HOT PEPPER PEACH COMPOUND BUTTER

2 pounds salmon filets, 1" thick, skin removed

¼ cup fresh lemon juice

1 tablespoon Robert Rothschild Apricot Ginger Mustard

Salt and freshly ground pepper to taste

¼ cup extra virgin olive oil

24 wooden skewers, soaked in water

* * * * * *

½ cup unsalted butter, softened

⅓ cup Robert Rothschild Hot Pepper Peach Preserves

* * * * * *

1 tablespoon fresh parsley, chopped

1 tablespoon fresh tarragon, chopped

1. Place the salmon filets in a shallow pan. Rub your fingers over the sides of the salmon to check for any bones. If bones are present, remove them with tweezers.

2. In a small bowl, combine the lemon juice, apricot ginger mustard, salt, and pepper. Whisk in the olive oil. Pour the mixture over the salmon and marinate for 1–2 hours.

3. In a small bowl, combine the butter and the hot pepper peach preserves.

4. When you are ready to cook the salmon, heat the grill to a moderately high heat. Drain salmon from the marinade and season with salt and pepper. Slice salmon length-wise into 24 long strips and thread each onto soaked skewer. Lightly oil grill grate. Cook salmon on preheated grill for about 4 minutes per side or until fish flakes easily with a fork. Remove from grill to a clean platter. While fish is hot, brush generously with hot pepper peach bu tter. Garnish with chopped herbs.

Serves: 12

 CHEF'S NOTE

Use a well-greased pizza screen to grill the salmon because as it finishes cooking, it will become more difficult to remove from the grill grate.

VEGETABLES & GRAINS

MICHAEL V. DISALLE

GOVERNOR OF OHIO
1959–1963

Michael DiSalle served in the Ohio House of Representatives and in many positions in Toledo, including Mayor, until 1950. He served as Governor from 1959 to 1963, the first to serve a four-year term.

Photos courtesy of Barbara DiSalle Lindskold

16

MYRTLE DISALLE'S WALNUT WILD RICE

2 tablespoons unsalted butter

1 onion, chopped

2 teaspoons salt

1 cup wild rice

1 cup brown rice

¾ cup walnuts, coarsely chopped

2 tablespoons fresh parsley, chopped

1. In a medium heavy saucepan, melt butter over medium heat. Add onion and sauté until translucent. Add salt, both kinds of rice, and 4 cups of water. Cover and bring to a boil; reduce the heat to low and simmer for 40–45 minutes. When rice is tender, fold in the walnuts and parsley. Correct the seasonings and serve.

Serves: 8

CHEF'S NOTE

Kosher salt is my preference when choosing a salt for cooking. It has fewer additives and has more of a salty taste than regular table salt. The flakes of salt also tend to dissolve more easily.

Mrs. DiSalle enjoyed many teas with her daughter during her time at the Residence.

Photo courtesy of Barbara DiSalle Lindskold

DANISH SAUTÉED POTATOES
DANSK KARTOFFLER

1½ pounds new potatoes
2 tablespoons clarified butter*
1 tablespoon sugar
Salt and freshly ground pepper to taste

1. In a medium heavy saucepan, add potatoes to salted water and cover. Bring to a boil and then reduce the heat to medium and allow potatoes to cook until tender. Cool, peel, and slice the potatoes about ⅜" thick.

2. Just before serving, heat large heavy skillet over high heat; add butter. Add the sliced potatoes and sauté. Sprinkle potatoes with sugar and continue to sauté until potatoes are nicely browned and caramelized. Correct the seasonings with salt and pepper. Serve warm.

Serves: 4

CHEF'S NOTE

This recipe comes from First Lady Hope Taft's mother, Janet Rothert. It is a favorite of their daughter Anna.

*Clarified butter is wonderful to work with. It can be used to sauté at very high heat because all the milk fat has been removed.

CLARIFIED BUTTER

Place unsalted butter in a heavy saucepan and melt slowly over low heat. Remove from heat and allow to sit for 5 minutes. Skim foam (milk fat) from the top and slowly pour into a container discarding any milk solids on the bottom of the pan. Chill. Store, refrigerated and tightly covered, for about 3 weeks.

MASHED SWEET POTATOES INFUSED WITH ORANGE AND GINGER

¼ cup unsalted butter, cut into pieces

2 tablespoons garlic, minced

2½ tablespoons fresh ginger, minced

1 cup heavy cream

½ teaspoon salt

1 tablespoon brown sugar

½ tablespoon orange zest

2 pounds sweet potatoes, peeled, halved then cut in ⅜" slices

1. In a medium heavy saucepan, melt butter over medium heat. Add the garlic and ginger; sauté until fragrant (do not brown). Add the heavy cream and reduce by ⅓. Add the salt, brown sugar, orange zest, and sweet potatoes. Cover and cook over low heat, stirring occasionally, until potatoes are tender, about 25–30 minutes. Remove from heat. The potatoes will be so soft that all you will need is a rubber spatula to stir (mash) the potatoes. Correct the seasonings and serve warm.

Serves: 4–6

CHEF'S NOTE

Be careful when cooking with fresh garlic. If you burn garlic it will give off a bitter taste. Chopped garlic over medium-high heat cooks in less than a minute. Be ready to add your next ingredient.

GRATIN OF POTATOES
WITH SMOKED CHEDDAR CHEESE

1 clove garlic, minced

2 tablespoons unsalted butter, softened

* * * * * *

1½ cups heavy cream

1½ cups low sodium chicken stock

¼ cup Pillsbury Unbleached All-Purpose Flour

½ teaspoon salt

¼ teaspoon white pepper

4 cups smoked cheddar cheese, shredded

2 tablespoons fresh chives, chopped

3 pounds baking potatoes, peeled and sliced ⅛" thick

1. Preheat oven to 375 degrees. Combine softened butter and garlic. Spread all over a 9"x13" ovenproof dish.

2. In a large heavy saucepan, stir together the cream, stock, flour, salt, and pepper. Place on medium heat and bring to a slow boil to thicken. Stir constantly. Reduce heat and stir in all but ½ cup of the cheese (reserve for the topping). Stir until cheese melts; remove from heat and add the chives.

3. Ladle ⅓ of the cream mixture into the prepared dish. Arrange ½ of the potatoes in a layer over the cream mixture, season with salt and pepper. Pour in another ⅓ of the cream. Add the second half of the potatoes finishing with the remaining cream sauce.

4. Cover baking dish and bake in preheated oven for 30 minutes. Remove cover and sprinkle the remaining cheese over the top. Return to the oven and bake another 30 minutes or until the potatoes are tender.

5. Allow potatoes to set for at least 10 minutes for ease of cutting.

Serves: 8

CHEF'S NOTE

If your gratin has not browned sufficiently in the allotted time, simply turn on your broiler, place the gratin beneath the heat, and very quickly the casserole will be nicely browned.

QUICK HERBED NEW POTATOES

1½ pounds new potatoes, cut in quarters

6 cloves garlic, more if desired, do not remove the skins

Olive oil

Salt and freshly ground pepper to taste

2 sprigs fresh thyme

2 sprigs fresh rosemary

* * * * * *

Aluminum foil

1. Preheat oven to 375 degrees.

2. With a double layer of aluminum foil, create a packet for the potatoes.

3. Place the potatoes in a mixing bowl with the garlic; add enough olive oil just to coat the potatoes. Season with salt and pepper. Place the potatoes and garlic in the center of your double layer foil packet. Top with herb sprigs. Fold the foil over the vegetables; fold over the remaining 3 edges at least twice to seal.

4. Place foil packet on a baking sheet and place in preheated oven for 30–40 minutes or until potatoes are tender. Be careful of the steam when opening the packet. Discard the herbs, check for seasoning and serve hot.

Serves: 6

CHEF'S NOTE

This recipe is not only easy but great to do ahead. The foil packet takes on another element of flavor when cooked on the grill.

Photo courtesy of Toni DiSalle Watkins

This is Governor DiSalle
relaxing with his family
after his grandson's baptism.

MASHED POTATOES WITH PARSLEY AND LEEKS

4 tablespoons unsalted butter, divided
1 small leek, white part only, minced
2½ pounds potatoes, peeled and cubed
3 cloves garlic, skins on
3 tablespoons sour cream
1 teaspoon salt
Freshly ground black pepper
½ cup milk
2 tablespoons fresh parsley, minced

1. Melt 1 tablespoon butter in small skillet over medium heat. Add leek and sauté. Remove from heat and reserve.

2. Place potatoes and garlic in saucepan. Cover with water and bring to a boil. Reduce heat, and simmer about 25 minutes or until potatoes are tender. Drain. Remove skins from garlic. Mash potatoes and garlic in large bowl. Add reserved leek mixture, sour cream, salt and pepper. Combine milk and remaining 3 tablespoons butter and warm in microwave. Stir enough liquid into potatoes to make a creamy mixture. Season with salt and pepper. Sprinkle with parsley and serve warm.

Serves: 4

CHEF'S NOTE

Russet potatoes are the best to use when making mashed potatoes. Also, work lightly with the potatoes as overmixing will leave you with pasty and starchy mashed potatoes.

NEW POTATOES, FRESH CORN AND CARAMELIZED ONIONS

1 pound new potatoes

¼ cup unsalted butter, divided

1 large sweet onion, cut in ¼" slices

3 ears fresh corn, removed from cob

½ red pepper, cut in 1"x¼" strips

¼ cup vegetable stock

½ teaspoon course salt

Freshly ground pepper

1 teaspoon fresh rosemary, chopped

1. In a medium heavy saucepan, bring potatoes to a boil in salted water. Reduce heat, cover and cook potatoes until they are tender, not mushy. Drain, cut in 1" pieces, reserve.

2. While potatoes are cooking, sauté onion with 2 tablespoons butter in a large heavy skillet over medium heat. Sauté onions slowly to evenly brown.

3. In another skillet, melt remaining butter over medium heat; add corn and red pepper. Sauté until corn is just tender.

4. Add the potatoes and corn mixture to the skillet with the caramelized onions. Turn up the heat and add the stock to deglaze the pan. Reduce heat and scrape up all the brown bits on the bottom of the pan. When all the liquid has evaporated, remove from heat. Correct the seasonings with salt, pepper, and rosemary. Serve immediately.

Serves: 4–6

CHEF'S NOTE

This dish can be prepared in advance up to the point where you deglaze the pan with the stock.

Why use stock and not water? Number one, it deglazes the pan, which brings up an element of flavor, and number two, the stock itself adds to the complexity of the flavor.

MÉLANGE CABBAGE AND
NEW POTATOES WITH TARRAGON

2 tablespoons unsalted butter

2 medium onions, chopped

1½ pounds small new potatoes, cut into wedges

½ head green cabbage (12 ounces), cored and cut into ¼" shredded pieces

1½ cups low sodium chicken stock

⅓ cup heavy cream

1 cup peas

3 tablespoons fresh parsley, minced

1 tablespoon fresh tarragon

Freshly ground black pepper, to taste

1. Melt the butter in a large heavy sauté pan over medium heat. When hot, add the onions and cook about 2 minutes, stirring occasionally, until they begin to soften. Add the potatoes, cabbage, and stock. Cover and cook about 6 minutes longer over medium heat until the potatoes are almost, but not quite, tender. Remove the lid and allow stock to reduce until almost all the liquid has evaporated.

2. Before serving, add the cream and peas. Warm slightly to cook the peas. Add the parsley, tarragon, pepper, and salt to taste. Correct the seasonings. Serve warm.

Serves: 6

CHEF'S NOTE

If fresh tarragon is not available the standard substitution for herbs is 1 tablespoon fresh herbs to 1 teaspoon dried herbs.

GRATIN OF CAULIFLOWER WITH ZUCCHINI

1 medium head of cauliflower (1½ pounds) separated into large florets

2 small zucchini, cut in ½" slices

3 tablespoons unsalted butter, divided

¼ cup Miceli's Grated Parmesan Cheese

Salt and freshly ground pepper, to taste

⅓ cup breadcrumbs (preferably Panko breadcrumbs)

1 tablespoon fresh thyme, chopped

1. Preheat oven to 400 degrees. Spread 1 tablespoon butter all over a 2-quart baking dish.

2. In a large heavy saucepan, add cauliflower to boiling salted water. Cover and cook for 8 minutes. Add zucchini to the pot and cook another 2 minutes or until tender. Drain and reserve.

3. Sprinkle the bottom of prepared baking dish with 2 tablespoons of cheese and top with cauliflower and zucchini in a single layer. Season with salt and pepper. Combine breadcrumbs, thyme, remaining cheese, and 2 tablespoons of melted butter. Sprinkle over vegetables.

4. Bake for 15 minutes or until the breadcrumbs are golden brown. Serve warm.

Serves: 6

CHEF'S NOTE

Panko is a type of Japanese bread crumb. It is light and crunchy and doesn't seem to get soggy. I use them in place of fresh breadcrumbs.

Photo courtesy of Toni DiSalle Watkins

Governor DiSalle's grandson, Mark, was caught by a Columbus Dispatch photographer playing in the sugar bowl during a reception for Senator John F. Kennedy.

SAUTÉED CARROTS AND BRUSSELS SPROUTS WITH APRICOTS

1 pound Brussels sprouts, outer leaves trimmed, cut in half

2–3 tablespoons unsalted butter

1 medium onion, sliced

½ pound carrots, ¼" sliced

4 ounces dried apricots, sliced

½ cup vegetable or low sodium chicken stock

½ tablespoon sherry vinegar

Salt and freshly ground pepper, to taste

1. Steam or boil Brussels sprouts until fork tender, about 4 minutes. Reserve.

2. Melt butter in large heavy skillet over medium heat. Add onion and cook slowly until lightly browned. Add carrots and apricots and stir-fry about 1 minute. Stir in stock and cook covered until the carrots are crisp-tender, about 5 minutes. Uncover and add reserved Brussels sprouts. Cook until all liquid evaporates. Season with vinegar and salt and pepper to taste.

Serves: 4–6

CHEF'S NOTE

Vinegars or acids are a nice way to pique the flavor of a dish. Add enough to heighten the flavor but not too much to make it too acidic.

BABY PEAS WITH CUCUMBERS AND MINT

2 tablespoons unsalted butter

1½ cups cucumbers, peeled, seeded and cut in ¼" diced

3 cups frozen peas

2 tablespoons fresh mint, chopped

Salt and freshly ground pepper to taste

1. Melt butter in a heavy skillet over medium heat. Add cucumbers and sauté until cucumbers are softened. Add peas and continue to sauté for another few minutes, or until all the liquid evaporates. Add the mint, season with salt and pepper and serve.

Serves: 6

CHEF'S NOTE

If you can buy English (or Hothouse) cucumbers, do so. They are seedless and thinner which means they have better flavor and are not as bitter.

Photo courtesy of Barbara DiSalle Lindskold

Barbara DiSalle was the first Governor's child to celebrate her wedding in the Residence.

CORN PUDDING SOUFFLÉ WITH CHIVES

3 cups fresh corn (3–4 ears), removed from cobs, divided

1 cup milk

3 eggs, separated

⅛ teaspoon freshly grated nutmeg

2 tablespoons unsalted butter

1 cup leeks, white part only, chopped

3 tablespoons flour

⅔ cup white cheddar cheese, shredded

½ teaspoon dry mustard

½ teaspoon salt

¼ teaspoon freshly ground pepper

3 tablespoons fresh chives, chopped

1. Preheat oven to 375 degrees. Butter a 6-cup soufflé dish.

2. Place half of the corn and the milk in the bowl of a food processor fitted with the steel blade. Process for several minutes. Pour into a fine sieve and press out the liquid and discard the solids. Stir in the egg yolks and nutmeg. Reserve.

3. Melt butter in a large heavy skillet over medium heat. Add the leeks and cook until leeks are softened; be careful not to burn the leeks. Stir in the flour; slowly whisk in the corn-milk-egg mixture. Continue stirring and cooking for about 5 minutes. Remove from the heat, stir in the remaining corn, cheese, dry mustard, salt, pepper, and 2 table-spoons of chives.

4. Beat the egg whites until they just hold firm peaks; fold into the base. Pour the batter into the prepared dish and place the baking dish in a water bath filled half way up with boiling water. Bake until the soufflé has a golden puffy crown, about 1 hour. Garnish with the remaining chives.

Serves: 4–6

CHEF'S NOTE

When beating egg whites for a soufflé, you want the egg whites to be about the same consistency as your base. Overbeaten egg whites will not fold in properly.

APRICOT AND ALMOND MOROCCAN RICE

1 tablespoon olive oil

½ cup blanched whole almonds

1 onion, chopped

1 carrot, peeled and diced

½ teaspoon ground cinnamon

1 cup rice

2½ cups chicken stock

½ cup dried apricots, diced

¼ cup currants

2 teaspoons orange zest

½ teaspoon salt

Freshly ground pepper to taste

* * * * * *

½ tablespoon fresh chives, chopped

1. Preheat oven to 375 degrees.

2. Heat oil in large heavy skillet, and sauté the almonds over medium heat until lightly browned and fragrant. Stir in onions, carrots, and cinnamon; cook until softened. Add rice and stir until coated with oil.

3. Stir in stock, apricots, currants, orange zest, salt, and freshly ground pepper. Bring to a boil; reduce heat to low. Cook covered, about 25 minutes until liquid has been absorbed and the rice is tender. Sprinkle with chives and serve.

Serves: 4

CHEF'S NOTE

This dish would be a nice accompaniment with Mustard and Garlic Marinated Lamb Chops (see page 40), a fresh green vegetable, and Sister Schubert's Pre-Baked Dinner Rolls.

BARLEY AND WILD MUSHROOM PILAF

1 cup pearl barley
2 tablespoons olive oil
2 garlic cloves, minced
2 shallots, minced
1½ cups shiitake mushrooms, sliced about ¼" thick
¼ teaspoon salt
Freshly ground pepper, to taste
1 teaspoon fresh thyme, chopped
3 cups low sodium chicken stock
¼ cup fresh parsley, chopped

CHEF'S NOTE

Instant barley can be substituted. Reduce the stock to 2 cups and the cooking time to 10 minutes.

1. In a medium heavy saucepan, toast the barley over medium heat until fragrant and lightly browned, about 4 minutes. Remove from the pan and reserve.

2. In the same pan, heat the oil and sauté the garlic and shallots over medium heat until fragrant. Add mushrooms and sauté until mushrooms are softened slightly. Add the salt, pepper, barley, and thyme; stir to coat. Add the stock and bring to a boil. Cover and reduce heat to low. Cook about 45 minutes until all the liquid is absorbed and the barley is slightly tender but still chewy. Let rest covered for ten minutes. Stir in parsley; taste and correct the seasonings.

Serves: 4

Image courtesy of Barbara DiSalle Lindskold

President Kennedy sent this telegram congratulating Governor DiSalle's daughter on her wedding day.

John F. Kennedy and Dr. Martin Luther King. Jr. were two of the nationally prominent guests at the Residence during DiSalle's term in office.

PESTO RISOTTO WITH ASPARAGUS

1 pound asparagus, stems removed, cut in 1" pieces

1 tablespoon olive oil

½ cup onion, chopped

1 cup Arborio rice

¼ cup dry white wine

3–3½ cups low sodium chicken stock, heated

2 teaspoons lemon zest

⅓–½ cup pesto sauce

¼ cup Miceli's Grated Parmesan Cheese

Salt and pepper to taste

1. Cook asparagus in boiling salted water for 4 minutes. Strain and refresh in cold water, reserve.

2. Heat oil in large heavy skillet over medium heat and add onions and cook until translucent. Add rice and stir to coat with oil. Turn heat to high, add wine, and allow wine to evaporate. Reduce heat to medium-low and add about a cup of stock. Cook until liquid is nearly absorbed, stirring constantly. Add the remaining stock mixture, ½ cup at a time, stirring until each portion of stock is absorbed before adding the next. When rice is tender, stir in the lemon zest, pesto, and cheese. Season with salt and pepper to taste.

Serves: 4

CHEF'S NOTE

Once the rice is tender, I like to add a bit more stock. This way the risotto will still be moist by the time it's served.

MAIN DISHES

JAMES A. RHODES

GOVERNOR OF OHIO
1963–1971 AND 1975–1983

James A. Rhodes is the only Governor to be elected to four four-year terms, 1963-71 and 1975-83.

No one loved Ohio politics more than Jim Rhodes. He served as Auditor and Mayor of Columbus, Auditor of Ohio and Governor. He also owned "Jim's Place", a restaurant near The Ohio State University campus.

First Lady Helen Rhodes loved Christmas and made her own ornaments for the official Residence tree. She also enjoyed decorating the house for other holidays.

Photo courtesy of the Ohio Historical Society SC SC 2899

Photo courtesy of the Ohio Historical Society P95

Governor Rhodes loved the Ohio State Fair. Entertainers, like Bob Hope and Pat Boone, were invited to the Residence when they were in Columbus to perform at the Fair.

HELEN RHODES' HAM LOAF

2 pounds ground ham

1 pound ground pork

2 eggs, beaten

1 cup milk

1 cup cracker crumbs, ground fine

½ cup brown sugar

1 teaspoon dry mustard

¼ teaspoon freshly ground pepper

¼ cup vinegar

1. Preheat oven to 350 degrees.

2. In a large mixing bowl fitted with the paddle blade, thoroughly combine all the ingredients. Place in an 8"x4"x2½" loaf pan. Bake in preheated oven for 1 hour 15 minutes.

Serves: 6–8

CHEF'S NOTE

Serve this old fashion comfort food with Sister Schubert's Pre-Baked Buttermilk Biscuits.

Photo courtesy of the Ohio Historical Society P 95

Mrs. Rhodes was known for hosting large teas Mondays through Thursdays but never on Fridays. That was her day to go to the grocery and buy flowers for the whole house. She would spend hours in the kitchen arranging all of them. Nothing was ever held on the weekends. "That was family time."

APRICOT GLAZED HAM WITH
APRICOT GINGER MAPLE SAUCE

12–14 pound (bone in) cured smoked ham

Whole cloves

* * * * * *

⅓ cup Robert Rothschild Apricot Oven and Grilling Sauce

2 tablespoons cider vinegar

1 tablespoon Robert Rothschild Apricot Ginger Mustard

* * * * * *

¾ cup Robert Rothschild Apricot Ginger Mustard

½ cup Ohio maple syrup

1. Preheat oven to 325 degrees.

2. Remove all but a collar of skin around the shank bone while leaving a layer of fat. Score the fat into diamond shapes. Stud the center of each diamond with a whole clove. Wrap ham in foil. Bake ham for about 1½ hours.

3. In a medium bowl, combine the grilling sauce, vinegar, and mustard. Take ham from the oven and remove foil. Brush glaze all over ham. Increase oven temperature to 350 degrees; return ham to oven and continue to bake for another 20–30 minutes or until the glaze is bubbly and internal temperature of ham is 140 degrees.

4. In a serving bowl, whisk together the mustard and maple syrup. Heat and serve with ham slices.

Serves: 8–10

CHEF'S NOTE

Any leftover ham can be used to make First Lady Helen Rhodes Ham Loaf (previous page).

If you somehow over-sweeten a savory dish, try balancing it out with 1½ teaspoon of vinegar.

ASIAN HONEY ROASTED PORK

3 tablespoons sugar

2 tablespoons soy sauce

1 tablespoon hoisin sauce

1 tablespoon fresh ginger, chopped

1 whole pork tenderloin

* * * * * *

3 tablespoons honey

1. Combine sugar, soy sauce, hoisin sauce, and ginger in a resealable bag. Add the pork tenderloin and marinate for at least an hour or overnight.

2. Preheat the oven to 400 degrees.

3. Remove pork from the marinade and place on a rack in a heavy roasting pan. Place in the preheated oven for 30 minutes or until the internal temperature reaches 145–150 degrees. Remove from the oven. Brush the roast with the honey and place it back in the oven to glaze, for a few minutes.

Serves: 4

CHEF'S NOTE

Hope Taft provided this simple, but scrumptious recipe.

This dish is especially satisfying served with our Sesame Noodle Salad (see page 86).

Photo courtesy of the Ohio Historical Society SC 512

The Governor's Residence foyer during the Rhodes Administration.

PORK MEDALLIONS WITH MAPLE CURRY SAUCE

2 (10 ounce) pork tenderloins, trimmed and cut into 1½" slices

Salt and freshly ground pepper

1 tablespoon olive oil

1 cup low sodium chicken stock

1½ tablespoons Ohio maple syrup

1 tablespoon coarse-grained mustard

¼ teaspoon curry powder

2 tablespoons unsalted butter

1. Preheat oven to 375 degrees.

2. Heat olive oil in large heavy skillet over medium-high heat. Season pork with salt and pepper. Add pork to hot skillet; brown for about 3 minutes per side or until pork is browned. Remove pork to an ovenproof platter and cook in preheated oven until pork reaches an internal temperature of 150 degrees.

3. Place empty skillet over high heat. Add chicken stock and maple syrup to deglaze the pan, scraping up any browned bits. Reduce to ¾ cup, and stir in mustard and curry. Reduce heat to low and gradually whisk in the butter.

4. Add the pork medallions back to the skillet to glaze, correct the seasonings and serve.

Serves: 4

CHEF'S NOTE

To brown meat properly, make sure the meat is dry. To achieve this, you can dust with flour or pat dry with paper towel. If the meat is wet when you add it to a hot pan, it will steam and not brown (caramelize). It's that caramelization that gives your sauce the flavor it needs.

OHIO LAMB SHISH KEBABS
WITH LIMA BEAN COULIS

2 tablespoons fresh cilantro, minced
1 teaspoon ground cumin
1 teaspoon paprika
2 cloves garlic, minced
Freshly ground pepper
¼ cup olive oil

* * * * * *

1½ pounds boneless lamb, (preferably
    from leg) cut in 1" cubes

8 whole button mushrooms,
    stems removed
½ pound thick sliced bacon, cut in
    1" squares
1 red onion, cut in wedges
1 yellow pepper, cut in 1" squares

1. In a small bowl, combine first 6 ingredients. Season lamb and rub with cilantro paste.

2. Thread skewers with mushroom, lamb, bacon, onion and pepper (in that order). Continue until all ingredients are used.

3. Make Lima Bean Coulis (recipe below)

4. When ready to serve, heat grill to medium-high. Grill kebabs on hot grill for 6–8 minutes, turning once. Cook kebabs medium-rare to medium. Allow kebabs to rest before serving. Serve with Lima Bean Coulis.

LIMA BEAN COULIS

3 cups vegetable stock
16 ounces frozen baby lima beans
1 large garlic clove, minced

1 small fresh rosemary sprig
3 tablespoons unsalted butter,
    room temperature
1-1½ teaspoon fresh lemon juice

1. In a medium heavy saucepan, bring stock to a boil. Add the lima beans, garlic, and rosemary sprig and return to a boil. Reduce heat to medium and cook about 15 minutes or until beans are tender. Drain, reserving stock. Discard rosemary sprig. Transfer to a food processor or blender and add the butter and lemon juice. Process until smooth while adding some of the stock to create the right consistency. Correct the seasonings with salt and pepper.

Serves: 6–8

CHEF'S NOTE

I put this recipe together for Governor Taft because two of his favorite foods are lamb and lima beans.

MUSTARD & GARLIC MARINATED LAMB CHOPS

⅓ cup olive oil

¼ cup fresh lemon juice

1 tablespoon Dijon mustard

1 clove garlic, minced

1 bay leaf, broken up

2 tablespoons fresh thyme, minced

1 tablespoon fresh rosemary, chopped

Salt and freshly ground pepper

8 loin lamb chops, cut 1¼" thick

1. In a resealable bag, mix together the olive oil, lemon juice, mustard, garlic, salt, pepper, and herbs. Add the lamb chops, seal the container, and refrigerate for 2–24 hours.

2. When ready to cook, prepare the grill. Cook the chops until they are medium-rare, 135 degrees, about 5 minutes per side. The time will vary depending on the intensity of the heat and the thickness of the meat. Allow lamb chops to rest about 10 minutes to absorb the juices.

Serves: 4

CHEF'S NOTE

I like to serve the Apricot and Almond Moroccan Rice (page 29) and Sister Schubert's Pre-Baked Angel Biscuits with this dish.

Photo courtesy of the Ohio Historical Society SC 512

The Governor's Residence living room during the Rhodes Administration.

Sister Schubert's™

OHIO PROUD

GRILLED FLANK STEAK WITH
SUN-DRIED TOMATO PASTA

1–1¼ pound flank steak

Your favorite dry seasonings

* * * * * *

8 ounces linguine

1 tablespoon oil from jar of sun-dried tomatoes

2 tablespoons shallots, chopped

2 cloves garlic, chopped

¼ cup sun-dried tomatoes, oil-packed, chopped

½ cup fresh basil, chopped

2 tablespoons fresh parsley, chopped

⅓ cup pine nuts, toasted

Salt and freshly ground pepper to taste

¼ cup freshly Miceli's Grated Parmesan Cheese

1. Prepare the grill. Season the flank steak with your favorite seasonings. Grill steaks until medium-rare (about 4–7 minutes per side). Remove from grill and keep warm.

2. Bring salted water to a boil over high heat; add pasta and cook according to package directions. Drain.

3. While pasta is cooking, heat the sun-dried tomato oil in a medium heavy skillet over medium-high heat. Add the shallots and garlic, sauté until softened and do not burn. Stir in the sun-dried tomatoes and cook just until warm.

4. Toss pasta with the sun-dried tomato mixture; add the basil, parsley, and pine nuts. Correct the seasonings with salt, pepper and Parmesan cheese.

5. When you are ready to serve, slice the steak on the diagonal, very thin, and serve with pasta. Garnish with fresh basil sprig.

Serves: 4

CHEF'S NOTE

To help keep your pasta hot for serving, I place my colander over my pasta bowl, so when I drain the pasta, the hot water warms my serving bowl.

TOURNEDOS OF BEEF WITH HORSERADISH MUSTARD BEURRE BLANC WITH ROSEMARY POTATO GALETTE

4 shallots, sliced

1 cup dry white wine

1 tablespoon fresh lemon juice

¼ cup of heavy cream

1–2 tablespoons Robert Rothschild Horseradish Mustard

½ pound unsalted butter, well chilled and cut up

Salt and freshly ground white pepper to taste

* * * * * *

1–2 tablespoons olive oil

4 (6–8 ounce) pieces of beef tenderloin

1. In a saucepan, add the shallots, wine, and lemon juice. Bring to a low boil and reduce the liquid until almost all the liquid has evaporated (about 2 teaspoons). Add the cream and 1 tablespoon mustard. Reserve until ready to serve.

2. Strain the liquid, while pushing on the onions, into a saucepan. Warm the mixture and gradually whisk in the butter, one piece at a time. Continue to whisk constantly until all the butter has been incorporated. Season with salt, white pepper, and mustard to taste. Reserve in a water bath.

3. Season meat with salt and pepper. Heat grill to a medium-high temperature.

4. Make Potato Galette (recipe on next page). Keep warm.

5. Grill tenderloins about 4 minutes per side or until internal temperature of beef is 130 degrees for rare. Place potato galettes on serving plates and place beef to the side of the galette and drizzle with warm beurre blanc sauce. Garnish with chopped parsley.

CHEF'S NOTE

Grill marks make a professional presentation. Place steak on a hot grill for about 2 minutes. Using tongs, give your steak a quarter turn to create the second set of marks, resulting in a crisscross pattern.

TOURNEDOS OF BEEF WITH HORSERADISH MUSTARD BEURRE BLANC WITH ROSEMARY POTATO GALETTE

(CONT'D)

GARLIC ROSEMARY POTATO GALETTE

2 Russet potatoes, peeled and shredded

1 egg

1 teaspoon fresh rosemary, chopped

1 teaspoon fresh thyme, chopped

1 teaspoon garlic, chopped

½ teaspoon salt

Freshly ground pepper to taste

* * * * * *

3 tablespoons butter

1. Place potatoes in a clean dry towel. Fold and roll towel around potatoes, and squeeze out as much liquid as possible. Place potatoes in a mixing bowl and stir in the remaining ingredients.

2. Melt butter in a large heavy skillet or on a griddle over medium-high heat. Place 3–4 mounds of potatoes in pan, pat down galette to ½" thickness. Cook until galettes are crisp and golden brown, about 3–4 minutes per side. Drain on paper towel. Repeat with remaining potatoes.

Serves: 4

The Governor's Residence dining room during the Rhodes Administration.

Photo courtesy of the Ohio Historical Society SC 512

Veal Scallops baked with Artichokes and Lemon Cream

2 tablespoons fresh lemon juice

1 cup heavy cream

1 teaspoon chicken bouillon granules

Salt and freshly ground pepper to taste

2–3 tablespoons fresh tarragon, chopped

* * * * * *

4 large veal scallops, cut from the top round
or top sirloin, pounded thin

All-purpose flour or Wondra

2 eggs, beaten

2 cups fresh breadcrumbs

1 (15 ounce) can artichoke hearts, drained,
rinsed, patted dry

1 tablespoon olive oil

4 tablespoons unsalted butter

4 ounces Gruyère cheese, shredded

Chef's Note

Wondra is an instant flour made by General Mills. It is formulated to dissolve quickly in hot or cold liquids. It's great for that last minute thickening power. I especially like it for dusting meat.

1. Preheat oven to 350 degrees. Generously butter a large heavy baking dish.

2. In a small heavy saucepan, combine the lemon juice, cream, bouillon, and seasonings. Bring to a boil, reduce heat, and simmer for 2 minutes. Add 2 tablespoons tarragon and reserve.

3. Season the veal and dredge lightly in flour. Dip in beaten eggs and then coat lightly with breadcrumbs. Refrigerate in a single layer for at least 15 minutes.

4. Place a large heavy skillet over medium-high heat. When pan is hot, add some of the oil and butter. Add the artichokes and sauté until they just begin to brown. Remove from pan and reserve.

5. Add more oil and butter if necessary, and sauté veal in as many batches as necessary. Add oil and butter when needed. Sauté veal quickly about 1–2 minutes per side until nicely browned. Transfer to baking dish, overlapping veal if necessary.

6. Spoon cream over scallopine and sprinkle with remaining 1 tablespoon of tarragon, cover with Gruyère cheese. Bake for 25 minutes. Serve warm, garnished with tarragon sprigs.

Serves: 4–6

CHICKEN PAILLARDS WITH SMOKED MOZZARELLA, HERBED GREENS AND MANGO SALSA

1 tablespoon fresh lime juice

2 tablespoons extra virgin olive oil

Salt and freshly ground pepper

2 cups small watercress sprigs

⅓ cup cilantro leaves

¼ cup fresh mint leaves, plus some for garnish.

* * * * * *

6 (4–6 ounce) chicken breasts, boned and skinned, cut in half on the diagonal

2–3 tablespoons clarified butter *(see page 18)*

12 slices smoked mozzarella

* * * * * *

Robert Rothschild Mango Salsa

1. Whisk together the lime juice, olive oil, salt, and pepper to taste. Toss with the greens just before serving.

2. Place each breast between 2 pieces of wax paper and pound to ¼" thickness and season with salt and pepper. Heat large heavy skillet over high heat, and add the clarified butter. Quickly add the paillards and sauté for about 3 minutes then turn. Add a slice of smoked mozzarella on each breast and cook for another 3–4 minutes or until the chicken is cooked through. Remove chicken to a warm platter, and cook the remaining paillards using more butter if needed.

3. When ready to serve, place about ½ cup herbed greens in the center of each plate and add 2 overlapping chicken paillards. Garnish with mango salsa and some chopped mint leaves.

Serves: 6

CHEF'S NOTE

A Paillard is a thin slice of meat that is quickly sautéed or grilled.

Clarified butter is used to get the flavor of butter and the high heat needed to brown quickly.

SMOKED CHICKEN & APPLES WITH A MUSTARD SCENTED SAUCE

1 cup carrots, thinly sliced

¾ cup snow peas, strings removed, cut into thirds

3 tablespoons butter, divided

1½ cups Granny Smith apples, sliced thin

3 tablespoons shallots, minced

1½ cup chicken stock

1½ tablespoons flour

½ cup heavy cream

2 teaspoons Dijon mustard

Grating of nutmeg

Salt and white pepper to taste

2–3 smoked chicken breasts, skin and bones removed and cut into 1" strips

1. Bring 1 quart of salted water to a boil. Add carrots and cook for 2–3 minutes; add snow peas, continue to cook for another minute. Drain and refresh in cold water. Reserve.

2. Melt butter in large heavy skillet over medium heat; add apples and sauté until the apple slices are slightly softened and golden. Remove from pan and reserve. Melt remaining tablespoon of butter; add shallots and sauté until they are translucent. Whisk together the stock and flour until flour is dissolved. Reserve.

3. Raise heat to high and deglaze the pan with chicken stock. Add cream and reduce mixture slightly or until sauce is thickened.

4. Stir in mustard, nutmeg, salt, and pepper to taste. Add reserved chicken, apples, carrots, and snow peas. Heat until warm. Correct the seasonings and serve.

Serves: 4–6

CHEF'S NOTE

The smoked chicken gives this dish a robust flavor. If you can't locate it, regular chicken breasts make a fine substitution.

Serve over Sister Schubert's Buttermilk Biscuits.

Sister Schubert's™

HONEY GLAZED CHICKEN BREASTS

6 chicken breast halves, bone in and excess skin trimmed

½ tablespoon salt

½ tablespoon dried thyme

¼ teaspoon cayenne pepper

2 tablespoons olive oil

⅔ cup orange juice

2 tablespoons honey

1. Preheat to 425 degrees.

2. Mix the salt, thyme, and red pepper together. Sprinkle over the top and bottom of each chicken breast.

3. Place a large heavy skillet over high heat; when hot, add the oil. Add the chicken breasts to the skillet, skin side down. When the chicken has browned, turn over and place the whole pan in the oven.

4. Warm the orange juice and honey together in the microwave. Stir to combine. After the chicken has roasted for 20 minutes, pour this mixture onto the bottom of the roasting pan. Begin basting the chicken with the juice and pan drippings periodically until the juices run clear or until the breasts have reached an internal temperature of 170 degrees, about 10–15 minutes longer.

Serves: 4

CHEF'S NOTE

There will be a significant amount of tasty broth with this dish. I like to cook some Inn Maid Egg Noodles and toss with the remaining broth. Keep the noodles warm for about 10 minutes. This will allow the sauce to be absorbed. Chopped fresh tarragon adds the crowning touch.

CHICKEN BREASTS AND HERBS EN PAPILLOTE

2 tablespoons olive oil

2 shallots, thinly sliced

8 ounces mushrooms, sliced

½ teaspoon salt

Freshly ground black pepper

1 tablespoon fresh lemon juice

4 chicken breasts, boned and skinned

4 sprigs fresh thyme

4 sprigs fresh tarragon

1. Preheat oven to 400 degrees.

2. Heat oil in a heavy skillet over medium heat. Add shallots and mushrooms, stir to distribute the oil. Cover and cook until mushrooms are wilted, about 5 minutes. Uncover, add salt, pepper, and lemon juice. Increase heat and stir to evaporate all the liquid. Remove from heat; correct the seasonings and reserve.

3. Fold a piece of parchment paper in half to form an 8"x12" rectangle. Cut a half heart shape, leaving the fold intact. Open up the parchment to create a true heart. Next to the fold, on one side of the widest part of the heart, place the fat-trimmed chicken breast. Season and spoon some of the mushroom mixture over the chicken. Top with a sprig each of thyme and tarragon. Fold the other half of the heart-shaped parchment over the chicken. Beginning at the top of the "half heart," start sealing the packet by folding over and over all the way down to the point of the heart to create a tight seal. Place on baking sheet in a single layer.

4. Place in preheated oven and bake for 25–30 minutes. Place parchment packet on dinner plate, carefully cut open top (be careful not to burn yourself). Garnish by placing a fresh sprig of thyme and tarragon in the slit.

Serves: 4

CHEF'S NOTE

This is also a terrific preparation for fish. The results are moist, tender, and delightful. Serve with Sister Schubert's Pre-Baked Dinner Rolls.

Filet of Tilapia
with Asparagus and Almonds

8 asparagus spears, tough ends removed, cut in 1" slices

4 tilapia filets

2 tablespoons unsalted butter

1 cup mushrooms, sliced

¼ cup sliced almonds, toasted

* * * * * *

¼ cup Miceli's Grated Parmesan Cheese

1. Bring lightly salted water to a boil in a small pan. Add asparagus and boil for 4 minutes. Drain and reserve.

2. Wash and dry tilapia filets. Dust lightly with flour; season with salt and pepper. Melt 1 tablespoon butter in a non-stick sauté pan over medium-high heat. Cook filets on both sides until lightly browned or until fish begins to flake. Remove from pan and keep warm.

3. Melt the remaining tablespoon of butter in the sauté pan. Add the mushrooms and cook until they are lightly browned. Add the almonds and toss to warm them.

4. When ready to serve, place tilapia filets on serving plate, top with mushrooms, almonds, and asparagus. Sprinkle each filet with 1 tablespoon of Parmesan cheese. Serve immediately.

Serves: 4

Chef's Note

Trout is also wonderful in this recipe.

If you peel the skin on the asparagus it will cook more evenly and the color difference is dramatic.

COCONUT SHRIMP WITH
ORANGE HORSERADISH SAUCE

1 cup shredded coconut

1 cup crushed corn flakes

1 pound shrimp, peeled and deveined

Creole seasonings

1 cup flour

3 eggs, beaten

* * * * * *

2 cups peanut oil

* * * * * *

ORANGE HORSERADISH SAUCE

18 ounces Smucker's Orange Marmalade

⅓ cup Creole mustard

⅓ cup horseradish

1. To prepare shrimp, combine coconut and corn flakes. Sprinkle both sides of shrimp with Creole seasoning. Dip shrimp in flour and then in egg. Press both sides of each shrimp firmly into coconut mixture and refrigerate. This can be done several hours in advance.

2. For the sauce, combine the ingredients in a small saucepan and heat until warm.

3. When ready to serve, heat oil to 325 degrees. Cook shrimp in oil until golden brown. Remove to paper towels. Serve with orange horseradish sauce.

Serves: 4

CHEF'S NOTE

This recipe can serve as a very nice appetizer if you use small shrimp.

COLD POACHED SALMON
WITH TOMATO BASIL RELISH

SALMON

4 salmon steaks, cut 1" thick

Salt and freshly ground pepper

1 tablespoon unsalted butter

¼ cup shallots, chopped

2 cups vegetable stock

CHEF'S NOTE

Poached salmon makes for delicious leftovers. A green salad with cold salmon or a hot pasta entrée with salmon, fresh dill, and olive oil makes a pleasant meal.

TOMATO BASIL RELISH

6 ripe tomatoes, seeded and chopped

¼ cup Nicoise olives, pits removed, cut in half

2 tablespoons shallots, minced

2 tablespoons fresh parsley, chopped

2 tablespoons fresh basil, slivered

2 tablespoons fresh cilantro, chopped

Salt and freshly ground pepper

* * * * * *

Salad greens and grilled green beans for garnish

1. Preheat oven to 325 degrees.

2. Season the salmon with salt and pepper.

3. Melt butter in a large, heavy skillet. Add the shallots and cook over low heat for about 2 minutes without browning. Add the stock, and place the salmon steaks in the dish. Heat the stock on top of the stove until it almost comes to a boil. Remove from heat, cover, and place in the oven for 8–10 minutes turning once. The fish should flake easily when tested with the tip of a knife. Don't overcook or the fish will be dry. The fish will continue to cook when removed from the oven. Let the fish cool in the poaching liquid in the refrigerator.

4. Combine all ingredients for the relish in a small bowl. Correct the seasonings and reserve.

5. When ready to serve, place the salad greens on a dinner plate and then the cold salmon. Top with the relish and arrange the green beans around the salmon.

Serves: 4

THANKSGIVING MADE EASY!!

Planning is the key to a mouth-watering, relatively stress-free Thanksgiving meal. The turkey should be the star!

The following time schedule will hopefully take out that last minute, frantic crunch time. No holiday meal can be fun when your guests arrive and gather in the kitchen to pleadingly ask, "Is there anything I can do to help?" A planned meal will allow you to be part of Thanksgiving instead of the supervisor.

SUNDAY

Start Thanksgiving week off right by creating a grocery list and by purchasing all of the items that will be needed for your holiday gathering. Be sure to look for the distinctive green and black OHIO PROUD logo while you shop!

Make sure to purchase an Ohio-raised turkey large enough to feed all of your guests. The rule of thumb is one pound of uncooked turkey per person.

MONDAY

Fresh is best, but if you did buy a frozen bird, begin thawing it today. Frozen turkey, like all proteins, should be thawed in the refrigerator, and never at room temperature. For safety and superior quality, leave the turkey in its original packaging and place it in a shallow pan. Remember, a whole turkey thaws at a rate of 4 to 5 pounds per 24 hours. Depending on the size of your turkey, the thawing process could take 3 to 4 full days.

Don't panic if there aren't enough days left to thaw your turkey before Thanksgiving guests arrive. For speed thawing, keep the turkey in its original, tightly sealed bag and place it in a clean and sanitized sink or foodservice pan. Then submerge the turkey in cold water, changing the water every 30 minutes. The turkey will take approximately 30 minutes per pound to thaw.

For a "melt in your mouth" juicy bird:

#1 buy it fresh
#2 brine it
#3 don't overcook it

TUESDAY

No Thanksgiving dinner is complete without dessert. Tonight make the Pumpkin Crème Caramel with Maple Cream recipe *(see page 129)*, however leave the maple cream whipped topping for Thanksgiving Day.

WEDNESDAY

You're well on your way to the perfect Thanksgiving feast. By now, dessert is done and your turkey is thawed and ready to be brined. Simply follow the Brined Turkey recipe *(see page 54)*. Tonight you can also prep all of the ingredients for the Sautéed Carrots and Brussels Sprouts with Apricots recipe *(see page 26)*, making sure to place each ingredient in its own zip-lock bag. Today you make the stock *(see page 55)* for your sauce. Refrigerate overnight so that you can remove all the fat.

THURSDAY

Thanksgiving Day is here. Four to five hours before your guests arrive begin preparing the roast turkey. Now you can put the finishing touches on dessert. First prepare the maple cream whipped topping and plate the Pumpkin Crème Caramel. Keeping in mind you will need enough refrigerator space to store each dessert plate.

One hour and counting. Start making the Mashed Potatoes with Parsley and Leeks recipe *(see page 22)*. While the potatoes are simmering, remove the turkey from the oven and tent with foil. The final step is to finish the sauce/gravy and Sautéed Carrots and Brussels Sprouts with Apricots recipes. Also, have your favorite holiday helper ready to carve the turkey.

BRINED TURKEY

1 (14 pound) fresh turkey
4 quarts water
1 cup coarse salt
1 cup Ohio honey
3 bay leaves
2 cloves
1 cinnamon stick
2 tablespoons black peppercorns
1 clove garlic, smashed
1 bunch fresh thyme

1. Line large stockpot with a heavy, large plastic bag. Rinse turkey and place in plastic bag.

2. In another large pot, mix together 1 quart water (4 cups), coarse salt, and honey. Place over high heat and bring to a boil. Add bay leaves, cloves, cinnamon stick, peppercorns, and garlic. Reduce heat and simmer 5 minutes. Remove from heat and add remaining water. Let cool. When mixture is at room temperature, strain over turkey and seal bag.

3. Refrigerate stockpot with turkey in brine for at least 12 hours and up to 18 hours. Rinse and pat turkey dry before roasting.

DELICIOUS TURKEY STOCK

Turkey neck, wing tips, heart and gizzard
2 tablespoons vegetable oil
1 onion, chopped
1 large carrot, chopped
1 stalk celery, chopped
6 cups low sodium chicken stock
1 bay leaf
3 sprigs fresh thyme
2 sprigs fresh parsley

* * * * * *
All-purpose flour

Make the stock the day before Thanksgiving.

1. Heat the oil in a large heavy saucepan over medium-high heat. Cut up the neck, heart, and gizzard. Add to the saucepan with the wing tips and brown.
2. Remove from the pan and add the vegetables. Lightly brown the vegetables and add the meat back to the pan. Add the chicken stock, bay leaf, thyme, and parsley. Bring stock to a simmer, cover slightly and cook until the stock has good flavor, about 2–3 hours.
3. Refrigerate stock. When ready to use, remove congealed fat from the surface, and strain.

ROAST TURKEY

1 (14 pound) Ohio turkey, neck and giblets (excluding the liver) reserved for
    making turkey stock
Salt and freshly ground pepper
2 apples, cut into chunks
1 orange, peeled and cut into chunks
2 onions, cut into chunks
½ cup unsalted butter, softened
¼ cup fresh poultry herbs (thyme, sage, parsley), chopped
1 cup chicken stock

1. Preheat oven to 425 degrees.

2. Rinse turkey and pat dry. Season inside and out with salt and pepper. Pack neck and body cavities with apples, orange and onions. Truss the turkey. Combine butter with poultry herbs. Carefully separate skin from breast meat with your hand. Spread herbed butter under skin and on breast. Roast turkey on rack in roasting pan in oven for 30 minutes.

3. Reduce oven temperature to 325 degrees. Add chicken stock to pan. Roast turkey for 2 to 3 hours more, or until a meat thermometer inserted in fleshy part of a thigh registers 170 degrees, and the juices run clear when thigh is pierced. Transfer turkey to a heated platter, allowing it to rest at least 20–30 minutes. Discard string and keep turkey warm; cover loosely with foil. Pour the juices from the pan into a gravy separator and the fat will rise to the top. Pour the juice back into the pan minus the fat. Add your fat-free turkey stock to the pan. Mix together a slurry of flour and water, add to the pan. (Note: To make a slurry use 1 tablespoon flour to 1 tablespoon liquid.) Bring sauce to a boil, and thicken to your desired consistency.

4. Correct the seasonings, by adding salt and pepper and possibly some poultry seasonings. Enjoy an almost fat-free sauce!

Serves: 8

CHEF'S NOTE

The tricky part about roasting turkey is that the breast meat is done at 170 degrees and the thigh meat is cooked at 180 degrees. This is why it is important to place your turkey on a rack, to help circulate the air.

Turkey Vanderbilt

¼ cup unsalted butter
1 onion, minced
1½ cups mushrooms, sliced
1 tablespoon paprika
½ teaspoon salt
8 slices leftover turkey
8 slices good quality ham
1 cup heavy cream
Grating of fresh nutmeg
½ cup Miceli's Grated Parmesan Cheese

1. Preheat oven to 375 degrees. Grease a 9"x13" baking dish with Crisco Non-Stick Spray.

2. Melt butter in a large heavy skillet over medium heat. Add the onions and mushrooms. Sauté until softened, do not allow to brown. Stir in the paprika and salt. Spread in prepared pan, top with alternate layers of turkey and ham. Cover with cream and gratings of fresh nutmeg.

3. Bake in preheated oven for about 15 minutes. Remove from oven and sprinkle with Parmesan cheese. Return to oven. Casserole is finished when bubbling and golden brown.

Serves: 4–6

CHEF'S NOTE

This recipe comes from Governor Taft's maternal grand-mother. It is a tradition in the Taft family to make this dish the day after Thanksgiving, using the leftovers, of course.

LUNCHES & TEAS

JOHN J. GILLIGAN

GOVERNOR OF OHIO
1971–1975

Photo courtesy of the Ohio Historical Society SC 2690

Governor John "Jack" Gilligan served from 1971-1975 as the 62nd Governor of Ohio. He served in the Navy during World War II. He saw action in the Atlantic, the Mediterranean and the Pacific theaters. He won the Silver Star for Gallantry in action off Okinawa.

Jack Gilligan had been a Cincinnati City Councilman and a member of the U.S. House of Representatives before being elected governor. He is currently serving on the Cincinnati School Board, an elected position he has held since 1999.

During the Presidential race of 1972, Governor Gilligan gave a reception for Presidential candidate George McGovern. Midway through the event, Hubert Humphrey, McGovern's political rival, called and asked if he could spend the night. Both guests slept at the Residence that night. Governor Gilligan said, "In some way I think that was an historic moment." (and also a memorable evening . . .)

Photo courtesy of the Ohio Historical Society SC 2691

KATIE GILLIGAN'S WHITE HOUSE CHOCOLATE SNOWBALLS COOKIES

1 cup unsalted butter, softened

⅔ cup powdered sugar

2 tablespoons cocoa

1½ cups flour, sifted

1 teaspoon vanilla

½ cup pecans, toasted and chopped

* * * * * *

Powdered sugar

CHEF'S NOTE

Parchment paper is used throughout this book for one primary reason, it preserves your baking sheets. Continual greasing will build up on your baking sheets. With parchment paper there is no need for that step.

1. Preheat oven to 350 degrees.

2. Blend together all the ingredients in an electric mixing bowl using the paddle blade.

3. Form into 1" balls and place 2" apart on a baking sheet lined with parchment paper.

4. Bake in preheated oven for 12–15 minutes. Remove to a cooling rack, dust with powdered sugar.

Serves: 3 dozen

Katie Gilligan was a gourmet cook who often prepared the meals for family and friends at the Residence. During her tenure as first lady, she was a tireless advocate for the mentally ill.

Here you can see this recipe from Katie Gilligan in her own handwriting.

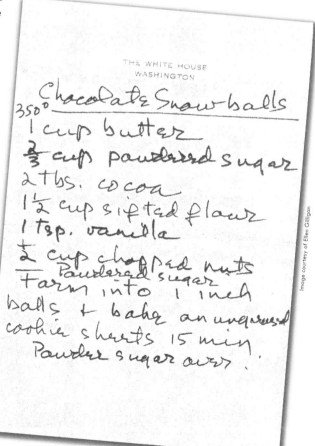
Image courtesy of Ellen Gilligan

SIMPLE SWEET SCONES WITH LEMON CURD

LEMON CURD

1 cup sugar

3 eggs

1 egg yolk

6 tablespoons fresh lemon juice

2 tablespoons freshly grated
lemon zest

½ cup unsalted butter, cut in 8 pieces

1. Whisk first 5 ingredients in a heavy medium saucepan. Place on medium-low heat and add the butter. Stir until the butter melts. Cook and stir constantly until mixture begins to thicken and the temperature reaches 160 degrees. Pour into bowl; cover and refrigerate until cold.

SWEET SCONES

2½ cups White Lily flour

1 tablespoon baking powder

1 teaspoon salt

¼ cup sugar

½ cup unsalted butter, cut in pieces

1 cup half and half

1. Preheat oven to 425 degrees.

2. Place flour, baking powder, salt, and sugar into a large bowl; stir to mix well. Add butter and cut in with a pastry blender until it looks like crumbly mixture. Add cream and stir until mixture forms a moist soft dough. Remove dough to a lightly floured surface and knead lightly about 10 times.

3. With floured hands, pat dough into a ½"–¾" thick large circle. Using a floured biscuit cutter, cut out scones and place 1" apart on an ungreased baking sheet. Brush with cream and sprinkle with sugar.

4. Bake in preheated oven for 10–12 minutes or until nicely browned.

5. Serve warm with lemon curd.

Serves: 8

CHEF'S NOTE

Frannie Packard served these scones at a tea hosted by First Lady Janet Voinovich for Barbara Bush. Mrs. Bush, mindful of the calorie intake, commented to Frannie, "You naughty little girl!"

Janet Voinovich visits with Barbara Bush at the Governor's Residence.

ALMOND RASPBERRY COOKIES

1 cup unsalted butter, softened

1 cup sugar

1 egg

1 teaspoon almond extract

¼ teaspoon salt

½ teaspoon baking powder

2½ cups Pillsbury Unbleached All-Purpose Flour

* * * * * *

Robert Rothschild Red Raspberry Preserves

ICING

1½ cups confectioners' sugar

2 tablespoons milk

Almond slices, toasted

1. Preheat oven to 350 degrees. Place parchment paper on baking sheets.

2. In the bowl of an electric mixer fitted with the paddle blade, cream butter and sugar until light and fluffy. Beat in egg and almond extract. With the mixer on low speed, stir in the salt and baking powder. Gradually add the flour until well incorporated.

3. Stir together the confectioners' sugar and milk in a small bowl and reserve.

4. Remove dough to a lightly floured work surface. Divide into 3 pieces. Roll each piece into an 18" long, ½" round log. Place on baking sheet 2"–3" apart. Drag the back of a wooden spoon handle along the center of each roll about ½" deep. Fill with raspberry preserves.

5. Bake in preheated oven for 15 minutes or until edges are lightly browned. Remove from the oven. While cookies are warm, cut bars 1½" wide. Drizzle with icing and sprinkle with almonds. Cool.

Yield: 4 dozen

 CHEF'S NOTE

This dough makes wonderful sugar cookies.

PECAN PIE BARS

CRUST

1⅓ cups Pillsbury Unbleached All-Purpose Flour

2 tablespoons brown sugar, packed

½ cup unsalted butter, softened

FILLING

2 tablespoons unsalted butter, melted

⅔ cup dark brown sugar, packed

½ cup light corn syrup

2 teaspoons vanilla

2 eggs

¾ cup pecans, chopped

CHEF'S NOTE

Indulge yourself and serve these cookies as a dessert. Cut the squares a little larger, and top with Graeter's Butter Pecan Ice Cream. Drizzle with warm caramel sauce.

1. Preheat oven to 350 degrees. Grease a 8" square baking pan with non-stick spray.

2. In the bowl of a food processor, blend all crust ingredients thoroughly. Press mixture firmly on the bottom of the prepared pan. Bake crust for 15 minutes or until it is lightly browned.

3. In a bowl, stir together all the filling ingredients. Pour over warm crust. Return to the oven and bake another 20–25 minutes or until the center is set. Cool and then cut into squares.

Serves: 16 squares

Gilligan dining room table dressed up for the holidays.

Photo courtesy of Gary and Kathleen Sebelius

FRUIT TARTLETS WITH APRICOT PASTRY CREAM

PASTRY CREAM

2 tablespoons cornstarch
1 cup heavy cream
2 egg yolks
½ cup apricot preserves, strained

GLAZE

¼ cup apricot preserves, strained

TARTLET PASTRY

2½ cups Pillsbury Unbleached
    All-Purpose Flour
Pinch of salt
⅓ cup sugar
1 cup unsalted butter, chilled,
    cut in 8 pieces
1 egg
½ tablespoon vanilla

* * * * * *

2–3 cups assorted fresh fruit

1. Place cornstarch in the top of a double boiler. Slowly whisk in cream and egg yolks. Set over simmering water and whisk until the mixture begins to bubble. Remove from heat, stir in preserves. Pour in metal bowl and lay plastic wrap on top of custard. Refrigerate until ready to use.

2. Place the flour, salt, and sugar in the bowl of a food processor fitted with the metal blade. Process to combine ingredients. Scatter butter pieces in processor. Pulse about 6, one second pulses or until butter is in chunks. Combine the egg and vanilla in a small bowl. Pour in the processor and process until dough forms a ball. Remove from food processor.

3. Pinch off 1 teaspoon of dough and place in each tartlet. Press dough evenly in the tart shells and trim the edges with your fingers. Place tartlets in freezer for 30 minutes.

4. Preheat oven to 350 degrees. Place frozen tarts on baking sheet and cook for 12–15 minutes or until lightly browned. Cool.

5. To assemble tarts, warm preserves. Spoon pastry cream in each tartlet; top with your choice of fruit and brush with warm glaze.

Serves: 12

CHEF'S NOTE

Invest in silicone bakeware for your kitchen. It has revolutionized the pastry world. The nonstick tart molds ensure excellent definition and foolproof release. Also, they can withstand temperatures up to 500 degrees. They are a must-have in a baker's kitchen.

If time doesn't permit, you can substitute Robert Rothschild Lemon Curd and Tart Filling for the pastry cream.

CHICKEN ALMOND SANDWICHES
WITH BASIL BUTTER

8 ounces chicken breasts, boneless and skinless (1½ cups ground)

1 small shallot

½ cup slivered almonds, toasted and chopped

¾ cup heavy cream

Salt and freshly ground pepper to taste

* * * * * *

20–24 slices whole wheat or white bread, thin sliced, crusts removed

BASIL BUTTER

½ cup unsalted butter, softened

1 teaspoon fresh lemon juice

½ teaspoon salt

½ cup packed fresh basil leaves, chopped

1. In a heavy saucepan, combine the chicken breasts with enough salted cold water to cover them by 1". Bring the water to a simmer. Poach chicken at barely a simmer for about 15 minutes or until there is no pink inside the chicken. Remove the chicken from the liquid and allow to cool.

2. Place shallot in the bowl of a food processor fitted with the metal blade. Process until the entire shallot clings to the side of the bowl. Break up the chicken and add to the processor. Process chicken to a ground consistency. Remove chicken to a mixing bowl, stir in the almonds and cream. The mixture should have a spreadable consistency. If not, add more cream to reach that point. Season with salt and pepper.

3. To make the basil butter, beat together the butter, lemon juice, salt, and then stir in the basil.

4. Spread a thin layer of basil butter on one side of each slice of bread. Spread chicken filling on one side of each sandwich. Cut into 4 triangles.

Yields: 40–48 sandwiches

CHEF'S NOTE

I like to use one slice of white and one slice of whole wheat for each sandwich. This makes for a colorful display when serving.

SMOKED SALMON CANAPÉS WITH PUMPERNICKEL TOAST POINTS

1 small shallot

8 ounces cream cheese, softened

¼ cup unsalted butter, softened

2 tablespoons fresh chives, chopped

2 tablespoons fresh tarragon, chopped

2 teaspoons fresh lemon juice

2 teaspoons fresh lemon zest

Salt and freshly ground pepper

* * * * * *

Olive oil

8 slices Pumpernickel bread

* * * * * *

12 ounces thinly sliced smoked salmon

Tarragon sprigs

1. Preheat oven to 350 degrees.

2. In the bowl of a food processor fitted with the metal blade, process the shallot until all chopped pieces cling to the side of the bowl. Add the next 7 ingredients and process until well blended. Correct the seasonings. Reserve.

3. Brush olive oil on both sides of the bread. Trim the crusts and cut each piece in quarters. Arrange bread in a single layer on a baking sheet. Bake about 5 minutes per side until bread is crisp. Cool.

4. Spread or pipe cream cheese mixture on each toast point. Top with smoked salmon and garnish with tarragon leaf.

Serves: 16 guests

CHEF'S NOTE

When making toast points, make a lot. They freeze well and are very versatile. You can use as many toppings as your creative mind will allow.

COLORFUL TOMATO AND GRILLED ONION TART

1 (9") pastry crust *(page 136)*

✳ ✳ ✳ ✳ ✳ ✳

2 large sweet onions, sliced

2 tablespoons olive oil

3 ounces Miceli's Shredded Mozzarella Cheese

3 ounces Gruyère cheese, shredded

3 plum tomatoes, sliced

1 large yellow tomato

Salt and freshly ground pepper to taste

¾ cup half and half

2 egg yolks

Freshly grated nutmeg

GARNISH

¼ cup Nicoise olives, pitted and chopped

Freshly chopped parsley

1. Preheat oven to 375 degrees.

2. Place in a large, heavy skillet over medium heat, and add the oil. When hot, add the onions and sauté until all the liquid has evaporated and the onions are a nice golden brown. Remove from pan to cool.

3. Roll the pastry to fit a 12" tart pan with a removable rim. Ease dough into tart pan, trim dough to a 1" overhang. Fold overhang into the rim and press to adhere to the sides. Spread onions out on the bottom of the tart shell and top with cheeses. Arrange the tomatoes decoratively in a circle.

4. In a liquid measuring cup stir together the half and half and egg yolks. Pour over the tart and grate with fresh nutmeg.

5. Bake in preheated oven for 30–35 minutes or until knife inserted comes out clean. The tart should be golden brown.

6. When ready to serve, sprinkle tart slices with olives and fresh parsley.

Serves: 8

CHEF'S NOTE

Caramelizing onions brings out their natural sweetness and transforms them into a sublime flavor in any dish. The trick is to patiently cook them slowly.

OPEN-FACED CHICKEN, BACON & AVOCADO SANDWICH

3 large chicken breasts, boned and skinned

1 tablespoon shallots, chopped

¼ cup sour cream

⅓ cup mayonnaise

1 tablespoon fresh tarragon, chopped

Salt and freshly ground pepper to taste

4 slices bacon

1 large ripe avocado

2 teaspoons fresh lemon juice

1 small baguette, cut in half lengthwise

* * * * * *

Robert Rothschild Honey Mustard

1. In a heavy saucepan, combine the chicken breasts with enough salted cold water to cover them by 1". Bring the water to a simmer. Poach chicken at barely a simmer for about 15 minutes or until there is no pink inside the chicken. Remove the chicken from the liquid and allow to cool.

2. Place the cooled chicken and the shallots in the bowl of a food processor fitted with the steel blade. Process the chicken until finely ground. Remove the chicken mixture to a metal bowl. Stir in the sour cream, mayonnaise, tarragon, salt, and pepper. Correct the seasonings and reserve.

3. Place the bacon in a heavy skillet over medium heat. Cook until bacon is crisp and nicely browned. Drain on paper towels. Peel and slice the avocado and toss with the lemon juice.

4. When ready to serve, cut out a cavity in each half of the baguette to create a space for the filling. Spread half the seasoned chicken mixture in one baguette and repeat with the other. Sprinkle with the bacon and top with slices of avocado. Cut into desired serving pieces.

5. Just before serving, drizzle the honey mustard over the top of the open-faced sandwich. Cut in serving pieces.

Serves: 8

CHEF'S NOTE

Open-faced sandwiches can be used very easily as an appetizer. Cut into smaller pieces!

GRILLED TENDERLOIN, ONION AND ROMANO BAGUETTE WITH SESAME MUSTARD SAUCE

3 pounds beef tenderloin
1 large Vidalia sweet onion, skins removed, cut in ½" slices
1 loaf French bread, cut in half lengthwise
2 cups Miceli's Shredded Mozzarella Cheese
½ cup Romano cheese, grated

* * * * * *

Robert Rothschild Sesame Honey Mustard Pretzel Dip, warmed

Fresh Italian parsley, chopped

1. Prepare barbecue grill (high heat). Place tenderloin on prepared grill. Brush onions slices with olive oil and grill until golden brown and softened. Turn tenderloin every 10 minutes until internal temperature reaches 130 degrees. Transfer beef to a clean platter with grilled onions. Allow to rest for 10 minutes then slice tenderloin thin.

2. When ready to serve, heat broiler in oven. Cut out a cavity in each half of baguette to create place for filling. Line each baguette with thin slices of meat. Top with grilled onions. Sprinkle each half with 1 cup of mozzarella and ¼ cup of Romano cheese. Place each half of baguette on a baking sheet and put under the broiler until cheese is melted and browned. Drizzle open-faced sandwich with warm sesame honey mustard pretzel dip. Cut in slices for serving and garnish with fresh chopped parsley.

Serves: 8

CHEF'S NOTE

If you don't want to pay the price for beef tenderloin, flank steak is a very tasty substitute.

Photo courtesy of Gary and Kathleen Sebelius

Governor Gilligan proudly gives away his daughter on her wedding day at the Governor's Residence.

ASPARAGUS AND CAMEMBERT TART

1 (9") pastry shell *(page 136)*

* * * * * *

1 pound asparagus, tough ends removed and trimmed to 3" lengths

1½ cups leeks, chopped, white part only

¼ cup vegetable stock

⅔ cup half and half

4 ounces Camembert cheese, cut in ½" pieces

2 egg yolks

1 tablespoon fresh tarragon, chopped

½ teaspoon salt

Pinch of fresh nutmeg

⅓ cup Miceli's Grated Parmesan Cheese

1. Preheat oven to 425 degrees.

2. Arrange pastry in a 9" tart pan with a removable bottom. Press dough into pie pan; fold extra pastry into the sides of the pan to create an edge. Pierce dough all over with a fork. Blind bake pastry by lining the dough with a piece of foil and fill with pie weights (dried beans or rice). Bake for 15 minutes. Remove from oven and remove foil with the pastry weights. Reduce oven to 375 degrees.

3. Cook asparagus in boiling salted water for 4 minutes. Drain and refresh in cold water. Reserve.

4. In a large heavy skillet over medium heat, cook leeks with stock until tender. The stock should evaporate. Pour in the cream. When the cream is warm, reduce the heat to low and stir in the cheese. When the cheese has melted, remove from heat. Allow to cool slightly.

5. Arrange the asparagus in a spoke-like fashion around the tart with the tips toward the edge. Stir the eggs, tarragon, salt, and nutmeg into the cheese mixture. Carefully pour over asparagus; sprinkle with Parmesan cheese.

6. Bake in preheated oven for 35 minutes or until knife inserted comes out clean and tart is nicely browned. Allow to set for 10–15 minutes before serving.

Serves: 8

CHEF'S NOTE

Blind Baking is a term used for prebaking a pastry for a filling that doesn't need to be baked. It can also be used for partially baking a crust with a wet filling, as in this case.

FRESH FROM THE GARDEN FRITTATA

9 eggs, beaten

¾ cup half and half

1 cup Monterey Jack cheese, shredded and divided

½ teaspoon salt

2 tablespoons unsalted butter

1 cup green pepper, cut in 1"x¼" pieces

1 cup grape tomatoes, cut in half lengthwise

4 scallions, chopped white part and tender green only

2 tablespoons fresh cilantro and chives, chopped

* * * * * *

Robert Rothschild Raspberry Garden Salsa

Fresh cilantro and chives, chopped

1. Heat oven to 425 degrees.

2. In a mixing bowl, whisk together the eggs, half and half, ½ cup Jack cheese, and salt.

3. In a 10" nonstick skillet, melt butter over medium heat. Add green pepper, tomatoes, scallions, and herbs. Sauté just to soften vegetables. Pour in the egg mixture. Allow eggs to set for a moment undisturbed.

4. Stir with a heat-proof rubber spatula from the bottom up; allow eggs to set. Stir again to prevent scorching. Continue until eggs are ⅔ cooked. Remove pan from heat. Smooth the top and sprinkle with remaining cheese.

5. Transfer pan to top rack of oven; bake until frittata puffs and the cheese slightly browns, about 7–10 minutes. Allow to rest 5 minutes before cutting. Garnish each serving with a dollop of raspberry garden salsa and chopped cilantro and chives.

Serves: 8

CHEF'S NOTE

This dish can be presented whole and looks impressive. Place a serving platter over frittata; carefully flip frittata. If you're having a really good day it will come out beautifully.

WALDORF CHICKEN SALAD WRAP
WITH DRIED CRANBERRIES

3 large chicken breasts, boned and skinned

1 tablespoon shallots, minced

1 large Red Delicious apple, chopped in ½" pieces

1 stalk celery, chopped

⅓ cup dried cranberries

¼ cup sour cream

⅓ cup mayonnaise

Salt and freshly ground pepper

⅓ cup walnuts, toasted and chopped

* * * * * *

6 spinach flavored tortillas

6 leaves of leaf lettuce

1. In a heavy saucepan, combine the chicken breasts with enough salted cold water to cover them by 1". Bring the water to a simmer. Poach chicken at barely a simmer for about 15 minutes or until there is no pink inside the chicken. Remove the chicken from the liquid and allow to cool. Chop cooled chicken.

2. In a bowl, combine the chicken, shallots, apple, celery, cranberries, sour cream, mayonnaise, salt, and pepper to taste. Correct the seasonings and the moisture of the salad. Fold in the walnuts.

3. To serve, place a lettuce leaf in the center of one tortilla, and top with about ½ cup of chicken salad. Fold top of tortilla over the salad, fold in the sides, and then roll up tortilla tightly. Repeat with remaining tortillas. Cut in half on the diagonal. Place half the roll down on the serving plate, stand the other half on its end so the salad is exposed.

Serves: 6

CHEF'S NOTE

For a charming lunch, serve these chicken wraps with Spinach Soup with Nutmeg (page 112), and the Governor's Apple Cake (page 127) for dessert.

SALADS & VINAIGRETTES

RICHARD F. CELESTE

GOVERNOR OF OHIO
1983–1991

Photo courtesy of Kent State University Archives Dagmar Celeste Collection

Richard Celeste served as
Governor from 1983 to 1991.
Early in his political career, he
served in the Ohio House of
Representatives and as
Lieutenant Governor. President
Carter appointed Dick Celeste
Director of the Peace Corps
from 1979 to 1981. President
Clinton appointed him
Ambassador to India
from 1997 to 2001.

The night he took office,
Governor Celeste wanted to
order pizza for a working dinner meeting.
Domino's didn't believe him when he said he was Governor because he didn't
know the phone number or address of the Residence. They hung up. He walked out to the
Highway Patrol to ask for assistance. "I gotta order pizza and I don't know how to do it."

Governor Celeste loved suspenders. While attending a cabinet meeting, Jack McCarthy,
Director of Purchasing for the Department of Transportation and Chef June McCarthy's
father-in-law, complimented the Governor on his braces. The Governor promptly removed
his suspenders and presented them to Mr. McCarthy complimenting his good taste.

DAGMAR CELESTE'S
MEDITERRANEAN MUSHROOM SALAD

1 pound fresh mushrooms, sliced, a variety of wild mushrooms are best

2 cloves garlic, minced

⅓ cup fresh cilantro, chopped

2 tablespoons balsamic vinegar

¼ cup olive oil

Salt and freshly ground pepper to taste

1. In a salad bowl, toss together the mushrooms, garlic, and cilantro. Whisk together the balsamic vinegar, olive oil, salt, and pepper in a small bowl.

2. Add some of the vinaigrette to the mushrooms and allow the mushrooms to marinate, at least 30 minutes.

3. When ready to serve, correct the seasonings and add more vinaigrette if needed. Place some greens on a serving plate and top with mushroom salad; garnish with fresh cilantro.

Serves: 4

CHEF'S NOTE

You will notice that in most recipes I mention the phrase "correct the seasonings." This is where you make the recipe your own, balancing the seasonings according to your tastes.

Photo by Steve Harrison, Department of Development

Governor and Mrs. Celeste had the Residence listed on the National Register of Historic Places and started a non-profit organization to help with the upkeep of the Residence. Since the Residence had been empty for eight years before they moved in, they were responsible for countless repairs to the property.

HONEY ROASTED CHICKEN AND NEW POTATO SALAD

VINAIGRETTE

3 tablespoons red wine vinegar

1 teaspoon Robert Rothschild Raspberry Honey Mustard

½ teaspoon salt

⅓ cup olive oil

* * * * * *

1½ pounds new potatoes

1 supermarket roasted chicken, skin and bones removed, cut in 2"x½" strips

1 green pepper, cut in 2"x¼" strips

5–6 Roma tomatoes, cut in quarters, lengthwise

½ cup fresh basil, julienne

* * * * * *

Mixed greens

½ cup honey roasted peanuts, coarsely chopped

Fresh basil sprig

1. In a jar with a secure lid, add all the vinaigrette ingredients, shake vigorously and reserve.

2. Place potatoes in salted water in a medium heavy saucepan over high heat. Bring to a boil then reduce heat and cook until potatoes are tender, not mushy, about 15 minutes. Drain. When cool enough to touch, cut potatoes in 1" pieces. Place in a mixing bowl and toss about 3 tablespoons of vinaigrette with the potatoes. Add the roasted chicken and green pepper. The recipe can be made ahead at this point. Place in the refrigerator until serving.

3. When ready to serve, toss in the tomatoes, basil, salt, pepper, and enough vinaigrette to coat. Correct the seasonings. Place the mixed greens on a serving platter and mound the chicken salad in the center. Sprinkle with peanuts and top with a basil sprig.

Serves: 4–6

CHEF'S NOTE

Julienne means to cut foods in very thin strips.

Reserve some vinaigrette for leftover salad.

TROPICAL PORK TENDERLOIN SALAD

2 teaspoons salt

½ teaspoons freshly ground pepper

1 teaspoon ground cumin

1 teaspoon chili powder

1 teaspoon cinnamon

2 pork tenderloins

* * * * * *

VINAIGRETTE

3 tablespoons fresh lime juice

2 tablespoons fresh orange juice

1 teaspoon Dijon mustard

1 teaspoon curry powder

½ teaspoon salt

¼ teaspoon freshly ground pepper

½ cup olive oil

* * * * * *

3 navel oranges

6 cups mixed fresh greens

1 red pepper, cut in thin strips

½ cup golden raisins

2 firm-ripe avocados

1. Preheat grill to highest heat.

2. Toast cumin, chili powder, and cinnamon in a dry heavy skillet over medium heat, stirring, until fragrant and a shade darker.

3. In a small bowl, stir together the salt, pepper, cumin, chili powder, and cinnamon. Coat pork with spice rub. This can be done 24 hours in advance.

4. Add all the vinaigrette ingredients to a jar with a tight fitting lid. Shake vigorously to emulsify. Reserve.

5. Place pork on a well-greased grill, reduce heat to medium and grill until pork reaches 145 degrees, turning every 5 minutes. Place on a clean platter and tent with foil until ready to use.

6. Cut peel off oranges including white pith. Slice oranges ¼" thick, crosswise. Toss greens with bell pepper, raisins, and enough vinaigrette to coat. Halve, pit, and peel avocados. Cut diagonally in ¼" slices.

7. To assemble, line decorative platter with dressed salad. Arrange ½" sliced pork, oranges, and avocados over salad. Drizzle with vinaigrette and reserved pork juices.

Serves: 6–8

CHEF'S NOTE

A trick in applying spice rubs is to lay a piece of plastic wrap on your counter and place the meat on the plastic wrap. Apply the spice rub; then roll the meat around to catch all remaining rub. Wrap meat in plastic to marinate.

SUMMER'S BEST CORN SALAD

4 ears fresh corn, blanched for 2 minutes
and kernels removed from cob

2 stalks celery, diced

1 cup grape tomatoes, cut in half lengthwise

¼ cup green onions, chopped

½ cup cucumber, seeded and
cut in ½" dice

1 green pepper, cut in ½" dice

Salt and freshly ground pepper to taste

⅓ cup fresh cilantro, chopped

* * * * * *

3 tablespoons fresh lemon or lime juice

¼ cup olive oil

1 medium garlic clove, minced

CHEF'S NOTE

To chop peppers efficiently, cut off the top and bottom of the pepper, stand it up and make a lengthwise cut from top to bottom. Lay the pepper down on your cutting board and cut out all the inside membranes. Cut lengthwise strips; turn and chop into desired pieces.

1. In a mixing bowl, combine the corn, celery, tomatoes, green onions, cucumber, and green pepper. Season with salt, pepper, and the cilantro.

2. In a small jar, add the lemon juice, olive oil, and garlic. Close the jar and shake until the vinaigrette is emulsified. Pour over the corn salad and combine until evenly distributed. Correct the seasonings and chill until ready to serve.

3. To serve, place some large lettuce leaves in a bowl or on a platter and spoon the salad onto the center; garnish with more cilantro.

Serves: 4–6

First Lady Dagmar Celeste was noted for her work in peace education and was delighted when Alfred Tibor presented the Residence with his sculpture, "To Life," which is dedicated to the children who lost their lives in the Holocaust.

STILTON CAESAR SALAD

¾ cup olive oil

2 cloves garlic, smashed

2 cups Italian or French bread, cut ½" thick cubes

* * * * * *

½ teaspoon anchovy paste

½ cup Stilton blue cheese

½ teaspoon coarse salt

1 teaspoon fresh lemon zest

¼ cup fresh lemon juice

Salt and freshly ground pepper

1 head romaine lettuce, cleaned, dried and torn into bite-size pieces

¾ cup walnuts, toasted and coarsely chopped

1. Add garlic to olive oil and set aside.

2. Preheat oven to 350 degrees.

3. Toss bread cubes with ¼ cup garlic oil, salt, and pepper to taste. Place on baking sheet and bake until golden brown, about 10–15 minutes. Cool and reserve.

4. Remove garlic from remaining oil and place garlic in the bowl of a food processor fitted with the steel blade and process. Add the anchovy paste, blue cheese, salt, lemon zest, juice, salt, and pepper. Process to combine. Add the remaining ½ cup garlic oil through the feed tube of the food processor and process until all the oil is absorbed. Correct the seasonings.

5. When ready to serve, toss the greens with enough of the vinaigrette to moisten the lettuce. Place in a serving bowl, top with croutons and walnuts.

Serves: 8

CHEF'S NOTE

After you bake the croutons, allow them to sit at room temperature to continue to dry. Any remaining croutons can be placed in a resealable bag and stored at room temperature. They are a wonderful addition to your pantry.

If you prefer not to make your own croutons, T. Marzetti's Large Cut Caesar Croutons would be a nice substitute.

GREEN BEAN, GRAPE TOMATO AND TORTELLINI SALAD

1 (7 ounce) package fresh tortellini

1½ pounds green beans, stems removed

¼ cup fresh lemon juice,

½ cup olive oil

2 teaspoons Dijon mustard

1 large clove garlic, minced

1 teaspoon salt

1 teaspoon freshly ground pepper

1 pint grape tomatoes

6 slices bacon, cooked, drained and minced

¼–½ cup fresh dill, chopped

CHEF'S NOTE

A vinaigrette can cause green vegetables to turn a drab green color. If making this salad ahead of time, toss the tomatoes and warm tortellini with some of the vinaigrette. Just before serving, add in the green beans and the rest of the ingredients with the reserved mixture.

1. Place tortellini in a large pot filled with boiling salted water. Boil according to package directions. Drain and reserve.

2. Refill pot; cook green beans in boiling salted water over high heat. Cook 5 minutes, drain, refresh in cold water. Dry with a cotton towel. Reserve.

3. In a jar, add the lemon juice, olive oil, mustard, garlic, salt, and pepper. Place lid on jar and shake vigorously; reserve.

4. Just before serving, combine the green beans, cherry tomatoes, tortellini, chopped bacon, ¼ cup dill, and enough vinaigrette to coat. Correct the seasonings by adding salt, pepper, dill, and possibly more vinaigrette.

Serves: 8

Photo courtesy of the Ohio Historical Society State Archives AV 4161

In 1984, Governor Celeste held a pig roast for Walter Mondale for 1000 people. It was a huge success. The Governor recalls, "Even today—25 years later—I have members of the national press corps comment on the pig roast for Fritz in the backyard."

CURRIED RICE AND CHICKEN SALAD WITH CASHEWS

1½ cups rice

½ cup plus 1 tablespoon olive oil

1 large onion, chopped

1–2 teaspoons curry powder

3 chicken breast halves, boneless and skinless, cut in 2"x½" strips

1 (10 ounce) package frozen baby peas

1 (7 ounce) jar roasted red peppers, drained and chopped

½ cup currants, soaked in warm water, drained

½ cup fresh cilantro, chopped

½–¾ cup cashews, coarsely chopped

* * * * * *

VINAIGRETTE

⅓ cup white wine vinegar

½ tablespoon ground cumin

Salt and freshly ground pepper

* * * * * *

Juice of one lime

Boston leaf lettuce

1. Cook rice according to package directions and cool.

2. Heat 1 tablespoon of oil in a large heavy skillet over medium heat. Add onion and curry and sauté till translucent. Add the chicken and sauté until cooked through. Transfer to a large bowl and cool.

3. Whisk together the remaining ½ cup oil, vinegar, and cumin for the vinaigrette.

4. Mix together the rice with the chicken mixture; add the peas, red pepper, currants, cilantro, and cashews. Add enough dressing to taste. Correct the seasonings with salt, pepper, and the fresh lime juice. Cover and refrigerate until serving.

5. To garnish, serve in a shallow bowl lined with Boston leaf lettuce and garnish rice with cilantro.

Serves: 8–10

CHEF'S NOTE

A roasted chicken from the store can be substituted for the chicken breasts if life is a bit too hectic for you.

Serve some hot Sister Schubert's Dinner Yeast Rolls with this salad.

Brown Rice Salad with Ham and Lima Beans

2½ cups low sodium chicken stock
1 cup brown rice
1 large carrot, peeled and diced
¾ cup fresh or frozen lima beans
1 cup fresh corn kernels
1 large garlic clove
⅓ cup fresh lemon juice
¼ cup fresh Italian parsley, chopped
⅓ cup fresh basil, chopped
Salt and freshly ground pepper
⅓ cup olive oil

¼ cup scallions, chopped, white
    part only
1 green pepper, diced
8 ounces good quality ham, slivered

* * * * * *

Garnishes

Romaine lettuce leaves
2 ripe Roma tomatoes, cored and cut
    into wedges
Fresh basil sprigs

1. Add stock and rice in a heavy medium saucepan and bring to a boil. Cover slightly and reduce heat to medium-low. Cook until rice is tender about 45 minutes. Don't over-cook or rice will become sticky. Cool.

2. Steam or boil carrots and lima beans for about 4 minutes. Add the corn and cook another 2 minutes. Remove from heat and rinse in cold water to stop the cooking. Drain and chill.

3. Place the garlic in the bowl of a food processor fitted with the steel blade and process until the garlic clings to the sides of the bowl. Add the lemon juice, parsley, basil, salt, and pepper. With the machine running, gradually add the olive oil through the feed tube.

4. When ready to serve, toss together the rice, vegetables, vinaigrette, scallions, green pepper, and ham in a large bowl. Correct the seasonings.

5. Place romaine leaves decoratively around serving platter, top with salad, and garnish with tomatoes and basil.

Serves: 8

Chef's Note

While the rice is still warm, add some of the vinaigrette. The rice will absorb the vinaigrette more readily, therefore making the salad more flavorful. Use this step when making pasta and potato salads.

ORZO SALAD WITH ASPARAGUS, BASIL AND FETA

1 cup uncooked orzo (rice shaped pasta)

1 pound asparagus, snap off tough ends and cut in 1" pieces

1 cup sugar snap peas, cut in thirds

⅓ cup diced red onion, soaked in ice water

¼ cup fresh parsley, chopped

¼ cup fresh basil, chopped

1 tablespoon fresh oregano, chopped

* * * * * *

2 tablespoons fresh lemon juice

2 tablespoons olive oil

Salt and freshly ground pepper to taste

* * * * * *

1 cup grape tomatoes, cut in half lengthwise

1 (6 ounce) package fresh baby spinach

⅓ cup crumbled feta cheese

¼ cup pitted kalamata olives, chopped

CHEF'S NOTE

Onions will become milder in taste if you soak the onions in 4 cups ice water with 1 tablespoon white vinegar for about 30 minutes. Drain and rinse.

1. Cook orzo according to package directions and add the asparagus and sugar snap peas during the last 3 minutes of cooking. Rinse in cold water to stop the cooking; drain well. Combine orzo, asparagus, and sugar snap peas with the drained onion and fresh herbs in a large bowl; toss well.

2. Combine lemon juice, olive oil, salt, and pepper and beat well with a whisk. Stir into orzo mixture; add tomato.

3. Place all of the spinach on a serving platter. Add the orzo salad in the center of the spinach. Top with feta cheese and olives.

4. Garnish with a fresh sprig of basil.

Serves: 4–6

Photo by Steve Harrison, Department of Development

The Governor's Residence living room during the Celeste administration.

SESAME NOODLE SALAD

VINAIGRETTE

⅓ cup soy sauce

2 tablespoons rice vinegar

1 tablespoon sesame oil

1 tablespoon sugar

½ teaspoon dried red pepper flakes, optional

1 teaspoon garlic, chopped

2 teaspoons fresh ginger, peeled and grated

* * * * * *

12 ounces linguine

4 ounces snow peas, trimmed and cut in 1" pieces on the diagonal

1 cup carrot, shredded

4 scallions, minced, white part only

½ cup fresh cilantro, chopped

2 tablespoons sesame seeds, toasted*

1. Add all the ingredients for the vinaigrette in a jar with a tight fitting lid. Shake vigorously. Reserve.

2. Place a large heavy stockpot filled with salted water over high heat. When the water comes to a boil, add the linguine. Cook according to package directions. Add the snow peas to the linguine the last 2 minutes of cooking. Drain the pasta and snow peas together. Toss the pasta with the vinaigrette, carrots, scallions, cilantro, and sesame seeds.

3. Cool salad in refrigerator, correct the seasonings, and garnish with chopped cilantro and sesame seeds.

Serves: 6

CHEF'S NOTE

* Toast sesame seeds in a dry heavy skillet over medium heat. Stir until fragrant and lightly browned.

T. Marzetti's Asian Sesame Salad Accents would be a nice addition to this salad.

We all love to throw together a quick tossed salad. What takes that salad from okay to great is the vinaigrette. Here are a few to do just that.

AUTUMN PEAR VINAIGRETTE

1 very ripe pear, peeled, cored
    and coarsely chopped
2½ tablespoons fresh lemon juice
2 teaspoons honey mustard
2 teaspoons brown sugar
½ cup olive oil
Salt and freshly ground
    pepper to taste

Place pear, lemon juice, honey mustard, brown sugar, salt and pepper in the bowl of a food processor or a blender. Process until the pear is pureed and the ingredients are mixed. With the motor running, pour the olive oil through the feed tube. Pulse until the oil is completely emulsified. Correct the seasonings.

Yield: 1 cup

ORANGE BALSAMIC VINAIGRETTE

2 tablespoons white balsamic vinegar
2 tablespoons fresh orange juice
1 teaspoon Dijon mustard
2 teaspoons fresh orange zest
¼ cup olive oil
Salt and freshly ground pepper to taste

Place all ingredients in an appropriately-sized jar and shake vigorously. Correct the seasonings.

Yield: ½ cup

APPLE HONEY VINAIGRETTE

3 tablespoons shallots, minced
1½ tablespoons honey
2 teaspoons Dijon mustard
1 teaspoon coarse salt
½ cup thawed frozen
    apple juice concentrate
⅔ cup cider vinegar
1 cup olive oil
Freshly ground pepper to taste

Place all ingredients in an appropriately-sized jar and shake vigorously. Correct the seasonings.

Yield: 2 cups

CHEF'S NOTE

For purchased vinaigrettes, Girard's Champagne Vinaigrette and Marzetti's Honey Balsamic are two of my personal favorites.

BREADS & BREAKFASTS

GEORGE V. VOINOVICH

GOVERNOR OF OHIO
1991–1998

George Voinovich served as Governor from 1991 to 1998. He served as a member of the Ohio House of Representatives, Lt. Governor, and Mayor of Cleveland before becoming Governor and currently represents Ohio in the U.S. Senate.

Photos courtesy of George and Janet Voinovich

The whole Voinovich family came from Cleveland each June for a special birthday celebration for the Governor's mother.

90

GOVERNOR VOINOVICH'S FRENCH BREAD

1 package active dry yeast
1 tablespoon sugar
1 tablespoon coarse salt
2 cups warm water, 100–105 degrees
4–4½ cups bread flour

* * * * * *

1 egg white, beaten

> **First Lady Janet Voinovich**: *This recipe comes from our Executive Chef Frannie Packard. The Reverend Billy Graham was a guest of the Residence. After dinner he went into the kitchen and told Frannie: "This is the best bread I've ever eaten!"*

1. Place the water, yeast, and sugar in the bowl of an electric mixer fitted with the flat beater. Allow the yeast to proof (dissolve) about 5 minutes. With the mixer on low speed, gradually add salt and 3 cups flour. When the flour is incorporated, turn the mixer up to medium-high and beat for about 2 minutes. Reduce speed to low and slowly add about 1½ cups flour, ½ cup at a time, until the dough wraps around the beater and cleans the sides of the bowl. You may not use all the flour. The worst thing you can do to bread dough is to add too much flour.

2. Remove the dough from the bowl to a lightly floured board. Knead the dough, only adding flour when necessary, until the dough becomes tacky, about 2–3 minutes. Place the dough in a lightly greased bowl and cover. Allow the dough to rise in a warm, draft-free place until doubled in size, about 1½ hours. Remove dough from the bowl and fold the dough into quarters. Place dough back into the bowl, cover, and allow to rise another 45 minutes.

3. Preheat the oven to 425 degrees. Place the dough on a lightly floured board, cut dough in half. Roll into French loaf form. Place the dough onto a greased French loaf pan. Allow to rise, covered with a towel. When the dough has doubled, make 3 slashes in each loaf with a sharp knife. Brush egg white lightly over each loaf. Bake for 25 minutes or until a thermometer reads 200 degrees. Remove from the pan immediately to cool.

Yield: 2 Loaves

One Christmas, the boiler for the furnace died. A large truck, parked outside the dining room windows, blew hot air into the house through a large flexible pipe until the replacement arrived. The intensity of the heat caused the candles to melt. Governor Voinovich insisted on keeping those bent candles in the dining room for a long while after the furnace was fixed. He said it was the warmest the house had even been.

Photo courtesy of George and Janet Voinovich

SAUSAGE AND SUN-DRIED TOMATO STRATA

½ cup sun-dried tomatoes, oil-packed, chopped

1 pound Italian sausage, casings removed, broken into chunks

1 small onion, sliced

1 pound white sandwich bread, crusts removed and cut in 1" pieces

3½ cups milk

10 eggs

1 tablespoon fresh thyme, minced

½ teaspoon fresh fennel seed, crushed

2 teaspoons course salt

¼ teaspoon freshly ground black pepper

½ cup Miceli's Parmesan Cheese, freshly grated

6 ounces Miceli's Shredded Mozzarella Cheese

* * * * * *

Fresh Italian parsley, chopped

1. In a large heavy skillet over medium-high heat, place 2 tablespoons of the sun-dried tomato oil, sausage, sliced onion, and sun-dried tomatoes. Brown the sausage and onions then drain the oil from the skillet.

2. Place bread cubes over the bottom of a 9"x13" buttered casserole. In a large bowl, whisk together the milk, eggs, herbs, salt, and pepper until combined. Add the sausage mixture and Parmesan cheese. Stir to combine. Pour over bread cubes, cover and refrigerate at least 4 hours or overnight.

3. Preheat oven to 375 degrees.

4. Bake strata uncovered until puffed and golden, about 40 minutes. Sprinkle with mozzarella cheese and bake another 10 minutes or until cheese melts and is slightly golden. Allow strata to rest before serving. Garnish with chopped fresh parsley.

Serves: 8–10

CHEF'S NOTE

A way to keep foods from sticking in the skillet, is to get the pan hot first. Set the empty pan on the burner. Allow time for it to heat. Add the oil; it should shimmer while carefully adding the meat. It really works!

MUSHROOM, LEEK AND CHEDDAR STRATA

12 (½") slices French bread

3 tablespoons unsalted butter

4 cups leeks (both white and the tender parts of the green)*

8 ounces shiitake mushrooms, stemmed and cut into ¼" strips

8 ounces good quality ham, cut in ¼" cubes

5 cups half and half cream

12 eggs

½ teaspoon freshly ground nutmeg

½ teaspoon salt

Freshly ground pepper

2½ cups white cheddar cheese, shredded

¼ cup Miceli's Grated Parmesan Cheese

* * * * * *

Fresh Italian parsley, chopped

1. Preheat oven to 375 degrees. Generously grease a 9"x13" baking pan. Arrange the bread slices over the bottom of the baking dish.

2. Melt the butter in a large heavy skillet over medium heat. Add the leeks and mushrooms; sauté until softened. Add ham and cook another few minutes. Spread ham mixture over the bread layer.

3. Whisk the cream, eggs, nutmeg, salt, and pepper in a large bowl. Stir in 2 cups of the cheddar cheese. Pour over ham mixture in baking dish. Stir slightly to mix vegetables with cream. In a small bowl, mix together the remaining cheddar with the Parmesan. Sprinkle over the top of the strata.

4. Bake in preheated oven for 30–40 minutes or until a knife inserted comes out clean. Cool 10 minutes. Garnish with parsley and serve.

Serves: 12–15

CHEF'S NOTE

*Two points about leeks: Wash thoroughly and don't burn them.

To wash them, split leek in half lengthwise and run under warm water to remove any dirt trapped there. Leeks can be substituted with yellow or white onions.

GLAZED BREAKFAST MEATS

1 (16 ounce) package of link sausages

¾ pound kielbasa, cut into 2" chunks

¼ cup apple jelly

3 tablespoons hot sweet mustard

2 (6 ounce) packages of sliced
     Canadian bacon

* * * * * *

Fresh Italian parsley, chopped

CHEF'S NOTE

*Presentation is always important.
The glaze in this recipe is not only
tasty but lovely on the platter.*

1. In large heavy skillet over medium heat, add pork sausage links, the kielbasa, ¼ cup water, and bring to a boil. Cover and steam 5 minutes. Remove cover and continue to cook. Turning sausages often until water evaporates and sausages are browned, about 20 minutes. Remove to paper towels to drain. Discard all but two tablespoons of drippings.

2. Stir apple jelly and mustard into the drippings remaining in skillet.

3. Add half the Canadian bacon; cook until bacon is heated through. Remove slices to platter leaving glaze in skillet. Repeat with remaining Canadian bacon.

4. Return sausages to skillet; heat and turn sausage to glaze. Arrange sausages on platter with bacon. Pour remaining glaze in skillet over bacon and sausages. Garnish with chopped fresh parsley.

Serves: 8

Photo courtesy of George and Janet Voinovich

*Governor Voinovich loved the garden. On sunny
days, the Governor was known to move meetings from downtown to the backyard picnic
table. He invited elementary school children to
the Residence to help plant and later harvest
potatoes in the vegetable garden.*

"To Die For" Cinnamon Rolls

Cinnamon Rolls

2 cups milk, warmed to 105–115 degrees
2 packages active dry yeast
1 teaspoon coarse salt
½ cup sugar
3 eggs
½ cup unsalted butter, softened
6½–7½ cups Pillsbury Unbleached All-Purpose Flour

Filling

¾ cup unsalted butter, softened
⅓ cup light brown sugar
⅔ cup sugar
1½ tablespoons cinnamon

Glaze Frosting

1 pound confectioners' sugar
⅓–½ cup milk or cream
1 teaspoon vanilla

1. In the bowl of an electric mixer, add the warm milk and the yeast. Allow the yeast to proof (dissolve) for about 5 minutes. Add the salt, sugar, eggs, and butter. With the mixer on low speed, add the flour, 1 cup at a time, until rough dough forms. The dough will still be sticky, but you should be able to knead it. Remove dough to a floured board. Roll dough in flour and knead for about 5 minutes, using as little flour as necessary. Place dough in a lightly greased bowl; cover and allow to rise in a warm, draft-free place, until it doubles in size.

2. Preheat oven to 350 degrees. Grease 2 (9"x13") baking pans.

3. Divide dough in half, and roll each half into a 15"x10" rectangle. In a mixing bowl, thoroughly combine all the filling ingredients. Spread half of this mixture over each piece of dough. Carefully roll dough tightly from the 15" side; pinch to secure. Cut each roll into 12 pieces. Place 12 cinnamon rolls equidistant in each pan. (At this point you can cover the rolls, place in the refrigerator and bake them the next day). Cover and allow to rise until doubled in size. Bake for about 20 minutes or until rolls in the middle of the pan are cooked through. Stir together all ingredients for the glaze. While the rolls are still warm spread with glaze.

I wish I had some right now!

Yield: 2 dozen

Chef's Note

This recipe comes to me from my sweet, very culinary savvy sister-in-law, Tara Reeder. Trust me—the title of this recipe says it all!

Using dental floss for ease of cutting the cinnamon roll dough is a great trick!

PEAR STREUSEL COFFEE CAKE

STREUSEL TOPPING

⅔ cup light brown sugar

½ cup Pillsbury Unbleached All-
  Purpose Flour

1 teaspoon cinnamon

¼ cup unsalted butter

⅔ cup pecans, toasted and chopped

COFFEE CAKE

⅓ cup unsalted butter, softened

1¼ cups sugar

2 eggs

½ tablespoon vanilla

1⅓ cups sour cream

½ tablespoon baking powder

½ teaspoon baking soda

½ teaspoon salt

2½ cups all-purpose flour or White
  Lily Flour*

3 firm but ripe Bosc pear, peeled,
  cored and cut in ½" pieces

1. Preheat the oven to 350 degrees. Spray a 9"x13" baking pan with Crisco Non-Stick Spray and dust with flour.

2. For the streusel topping, in a mixing bowl, combine the brown sugar, flour, and cinnamon. Using a pastry blender, cut in the butter until evenly distributed. Stir in the pecans and reserve.

3. In the bowl of an electric mixer, beat together the butter and sugar until well creamed. Add the eggs, one at a time, beating well after each addition. Beat in the vanilla and sour cream. Turn the mixer on low speed and add the baking powder, soda, and salt. Turn mixer on high to thoroughly mix. Turn the mixer back down to low and gradually add in the flour while occasionally scraping down the sides of the bowl. Fold in the pears. Spoon the batter in the prepared pan and spread evenly. Sprinkle batter with streusel topping.

4. Bake in preheated oven for 45–50 minutes or until cake tester comes out clean. Cool on wire rack. Serve warm.

Serves: 15

CHEF'S NOTE

White Lily Flour is very popular in the South, especially for baking cakes, biscuits, and quick breads. It has a lower gluten/protein content than all-purpose flour and a bit higher than cake flour. It creates a light and tender baked product.

Overnight Cinnamon Coffee Cake

Coffee Cake

¾ cup unsalted butter, softened

1 cup sugar

2 eggs

1 cup (8 ounces) sour cream

1 teaspoon baking powder

1 teaspoon baking soda

½ teaspoon salt

1 teaspoon nutmeg

2 cups all-purpose flour or
    White Lily Flour

Streusel Topping

¾ cup light brown sugar

½–¾ cup walnuts, toasted
    and chopped

1 teaspoon cinnamon

1. In an electric mixing bowl, cream together butter and sugar until light and fluffy.

2. Add eggs, one at a time, beating after each addition. Beat in sour cream. With the mixer on low speed, stir in the baking powder, baking soda, salt, and nutmeg. Slowly stir in the flour until well incorporated.

3. Pour batter into a well greased 9"x13" baking pan.

4. In a small bowl, combine the brown sugar, walnuts, and cinnamon. Mix well and sprinkle over batter. Cover and chill overnight.

5. When ready to bake, preheat the oven to 350 degrees. Bake for 35–40 minutes, or until a tester comes out clean. Serve warm.

Serves: 15

Chef's Note

When I make coffee cakes, brownies, or anything that's difficult to cut out from the pan, I line the pan with aluminum foil before baking. To do this, turn the pan upside down. Form the foil over the bottom. Carefully remove the foil and turn the pan right side up. Form the foil in the baking dish and prepare the dish as directed. When your baked product is cool, remove the foil and cake from the pan. Fold down the foil and your cake will slice beautifully.

BAKED FRENCH TOAST
WITH BLUEBERRIES AND PECANS

1 (1 pound) loaf French bread, cut in 1" slices

8 eggs

3 cups half and half

⅔ cup light brown sugar

½ tablespoon vanilla

½ teaspoon cinnamon

¼ teaspoon freshly grated nutmeg

Dash of salt

* * * * * *

1 cup pecans, chopped and toasted

2 cups blueberries

* * * * * *

¼ cup unsalted butter

¼ cup light brown sugar

1. Generously butter a 9"x13" baking dish. Place French bread slices in baking dish, overlapping each piece and creating 2 rows. In a large bowl, combine the eggs, half and half, sugar, vanilla, cinnamon, nutmeg, and salt. Whisk together until thoroughly combined. Pour over bread in baking dish making sure the bread is covered with liquid. Cover and refrigerate overnight.

2. Preheat oven to 350 degrees.

3. Sprinkle pecans and blueberries over casserole.

4. Place the butter and brown sugar in a small heavy saucepan over medium heat. Melt the butter and stir in the sugar. Drizzle butter/sugar mixture over French toast. Bake in preheated oven for about 30 minutes or until puffy and lightly golden.

Serves: 8

CHEF'S NOTE

To make this dish even more tempting, place 1 cup Robert Rothschild Wild Blueberry Preserves and 1 cup maple syrup in a small saucepan over medium heat. Cook and stir until heated through. Serve warm with the French toast.

REFRIGERATOR BRAN MUFFINS

1 (20 ounce) raisin bran cereal

3 cups sugar

3 cups all-purpose flour or White Lily Flour

1 cup whole wheat flour

1 cup oatmeal

2 tablespoons baking soda

2 teaspoons cinnamon

2 teaspoons nutmeg

1 teaspoon ginger

2 teaspoons salt

4 eggs

1 cup Crisco Vegetable Oil

1 quart buttermilk

1 cup pecans, toasted and chopped

1 cup raisins

1. In a large bowl, combine the cereal, sugar, flours, oatmeal, soda, cinnamon, nutmeg, ginger, and salt. In another bowl, mix together the eggs, oil, and buttermilk. Add the liquid mixture to the dry and stir together until just moistened. Stir in the pecans and raisins.

2. When ready to bake, preheat oven to 350 degrees. Grease your desired muffin tin. Using an ice cream scoop, fill muffin tins ⅔ full. Bake for 20 minutes or until toothpick inserted comes out clean.

Yields: 3 dozens

CHEF'S NOTE

The beauty of this recipe is that it stays fresh in the refrigerator for 6 weeks. It is perfect for the Residence because there are times when the Governor will have guests for breakfast and the chef is not there. These muffins make for a quick and fresh continental breakfast.

RASPBERRY CORN MUFFINS WITH CINNAMON PECAN TOPPING

MUFFIN

1 cup milk

½ cup Crisco Vegetable Oil

2 eggs

1½ cups all-purpose flour or White Lily Flour

1½ cups yellow corn meal

1 cup sugar

4 teaspoons baking powder

1 teaspoon salt

1 teaspoon cinnamon

2 cups fresh or frozen red raspberries

CINNAMON PECAN TOPPING

⅓ cup light brown sugar

¼ cup Pillsbury Unbleached All-Purpose Flour

½ teaspoon cinnamon

3 tablespoons unsalted butter, cold

¼ cup pecans, chopped

1. Preheat oven to 400 degrees. Grease muffin tins with Crisco Non-Stick Spray.

2. For the streusel topping, combine the brown sugar, flour, and cinnamon in a small bowl. Cut in the butter with a pastry blender. Add the pecans. Reserve.

3. In a 2-cup liquid measuring cup, measure the milk, add the oil, and whisk in the eggs.

4. In a large mixing bowl, stir together the flour, corn meal, sugar, baking powder, salt, and cinnamon. Add the liquid ingredients to the dry. Carefully fold together just until the flour is moistened. Just before you reach that point, fold in the raspberries. Do not over mix!

5. Using an ice cream scoop, add muffin batter to muffin tins. Fill ⅔ full, and sprinkle streusel over each muffin. Bake in prepared oven for about 20 minutes or until toothpick comes out clean. Remove muffins to a cooling rack; serve warm.

Yields: 18 muffins

CHEF'S NOTE

There is no better tool for adding muffin batter to the tin than the right size ice cream scoop.

ENGLISH TEA SCONES

2 cups White Lily Flour
¼ cup sugar
1 tablespoon baking powder
1 teaspoon salt
3 tablespoons unsalted butter, cold, cut in pieces
1 egg
1–1¼ cup heavy cream

CHEF'S NOTE

Flour absorbs moisture from the air. That can throw the flour/moisture balance off. The amount of liquid you add will depend on the moisture content of your flour. A moist dough is important when making scones. Moist dough, moist scones!

The trick when making scones/biscuits is to make sure you have a wet dough. If your dough is dry, you may need to add more liquid. It doesn't matter whether you use cream or milk.

1. Preheat oven to 350 degrees.

2. In a mixing bowl, combine the flour, sugar, baking powder, and salt. With a pastry blender, cut in the butter until the mixture looks like meal. In another bowl, whisk together the egg and cream. Add to the dry ingredients. Mix together to create a wet, sticky mixture. Place dough on a floured work surface and knead lightly about 10 times; the dough should be a cohesive mass. Place dough on a well-greased baking sheet and press into a 10" circle. With a floured knife, cut dough in 8 equal pieces, like a pie, but leave dough intact.

3. Bake for about 15 minutes or until golden brown. Serve warm with your favorite marmalade.

Serves: 8

First Lady Janet Voinovich found furniture that complemented the architecture of the Residence in state storage facilities and at tag sales around Columbus. She and Governor Voinovich established the Governor's Residence Advisory Commission to maintain the historic character of the property. During her eight years as First Lady, she promoted the Adopt-a-School program, Help Me Grow, and breast cancer awareness.

Photo courtesy of George and Janet Voinovich

BANANA BLACK RASPBERRY BREAD

½ cup Crisco Vegetable Oil

1 cup sugar

2 eggs

4 ripe bananas, mashed

½ tablespoon vanilla

1 teaspoon cinnamon

½ teaspoon salt

1 teaspoon baking soda

½ teaspoon baking powder

2 cups all-purpose flour or White Lily Flour

* * * * * *

1 cup black raspberries

½ cup walnuts, toasted and chopped (optional)

CHEF'S NOTE

Toasting nuts intensifies their flavor and adds a crunch. And toasted nuts aren't as likely to sink in batter-based recipes.

1. Preheat the oven to 350 degrees. Generously grease a 9"x4" loaf pan with Crisco Non-Stick Spray.

2. In a large bowl, beat together the oil, sugar, eggs, bananas and vanilla. In another bowl, stir together cinnamon, salt, baking soda, baking powder and flour. Add the liquid ingredients into the dry. Carefully fold the banana batter into the dry ingredients. Continue until the dry ingredients are moistened. Fold in the raspberries and walnuts. Pour into prepared pan and bake about 1 hour or until toothpick comes out clean. Do not over bake.

Yield: 1 Loaf

Photo courtesy of George and Janet Voinovich

Governor Voinovich and Executive Chef June McCarthy with Hartmut Handke of Handke's Cuisine and Jim Budros of City Barbeque.

LUSCIOUS LEMON BLUEBERRY BREAD

BLUEBERRY BREAD

¾ cup Crisco Vegetable Oil

3 eggs

3 tablespoons lemon zest

¾ cup milk

2 cups all-purpose flour or White Lily Flour

1½ cups sugar

¾ teaspoon salt

½ tablespoon baking powder

2 cups fresh or frozen blueberries

* * * * * *

LEMON GLAZE

½ cup fresh lemon juice

½ cup confectioners' sugar

1. Preheat oven to 350 degrees. Generously grease 2 (8"x4"x2½") loaf pans with Crisco Non-Stick Spray.

2. In a large mixing bowl, beat together the oil, eggs, lemon zest, and milk. In another bowl combine the flour, sugar, salt, and baking powder. Fold the liquid ingredients into the dry. Carefully combine ingredients together just until the flour is moistened. Fold in half the blueberries.

3. Divide the batter between both pans. Also divide remaining blueberries over the top of each pan. Bake in preheated oven for about an hour or until toothpick comes out clean. Remove bread to cooling rack.

4. While the bread is baking, whisk together the lemon juice and confectioners' sugar. Pierce the tops of each loaf several times with a toothpick. Spoon glaze over loaves as soon as they come out of the oven. Allow time for the glaze to absorb, about 30 minutes. Remove bread from pan to a cooling rack.

Yield: 2 Loaves

CHEF'S NOTE

If using frozen berries in a baked product, make sure they are frozen when you fold them in; otherwise, they will bleed. You can also toss the frozen berries with a small amount of flour.

IRISH SODA BREAD

2⅔ cups whole wheat flour

1 cup Pillsbury Unbleached All-Purpose Flour

1 teaspoon salt

1 teaspoon baking soda

2 tablespoons sugar

4 tablespoons unsalted butter, cold

2 cups buttermilk

1. Preheat oven to 375 degrees. Butter an 8" round cake pan with 2" side.

2. In a large mixing bowl, stir together both flours, salt, baking soda, and sugar. Using a pastry blender, cut in the butter until small pieces are well distributed. Pour in the buttermilk and stir in until the dough comes together. This should be wet dough. Turn out onto a floured board. With a gentle touch, knead the dough about 10 times. Place in prepared pan, and push dough gently to fit pan. Score dough into quarters and very lightly dust with flour.

3. Bake in preheated oven for 50 minutes or until toothpick comes out clean. Cool in pan about 10 minutes and then remove to a cooling rack.

Serves: 12

CHEF'S NOTE

Soda bread is a quick bread; therefore, it will become stale very quickly. If you have any leftover, store in the freezer.

This is the soda bread you find all over Ireland. I found this recipe while on a trip there in 2004.

SOUPS

NANCY HOLLISTER

GOVERNOR OF OHIO
DECEMBER 31, 1998–JANUARY 11, 1999

In late December 1998 when Governor Voinovich became a U.S. Senator, Lt. Governor Nancy Hollister became the first female Governor of Ohio. She was Governor until January 11, 1999.

Nancy Hollister's first visit to the Residence was as Mayor of Marietta when Governor Celeste invited her and the Mayor of Cleveland, George Voinovich, to lunch. Little did anyone suspect that each of the luncheon guests would be a Governor of the state of Ohio. As Lt. Governor, she sat around that same table for Governor Voinovich's weekly senior staff meetings. As Governor, she served her family meals in the same place.

Governor Hollister's children and granddaughter enjoyed the Residence. They set up big toys in the front hall and went sledding on the hill across the street. Neighbors gathered to watch her children making snow angels in the front yard.

NANCY HOLLISTER'S POTATO SOUP

2 tablespoons unsalted butter

1 small sweet onion, chopped

1 large leek, white part only, chopped

2 cloves, garlic, minced

2–3 celery stalks, chopped

1 pound potatoes, peeled and chopped in ½" cubes

4 cups low sodium chicken stock

⅓ cup heavy cream

Salt and freshly ground pepper

* * * * * *

GARNISH

T. Marzetti's Restaurant Style Croutons

Freshly Miceli's Grated Parmesan Cheese

1. Sauté onions, leeks, garlic and celery with butter in a large heavy saucepan over medium heat. Stir in potatoes and chicken stock. Cover, bring mixture to a boil and reduce heat to a simmer. Cook for 25 minutes or until potatoes are tender. Remove from heat.

2. Place in the bowl of a food processor or blender; pulse until the soup is still slightly chunky with potatoes. Return soup to the saucepan, warm and add the cream. Correct the seasonings with salt and pepper. Serve with croutons and grated Parmesan cheese.

Serves: 8

CHEF'S NOTE

You will notice that I use only unsalted butter in my recipes. Unsalted butter has a fresher and better taste. Salt is used in butter as a preservative, therefore unsalted butter is fresher.

ROASTED VEGETABLE SOUP

3 carrots, peeled and cut ½" pieces

3 parsnips, peeled and cut in ½" pieces

3 celery stalks, cut in ½" pieces

4 small tomatoes, quartered

2 ears fresh corn, removed from cob

2 onions, quartered

1½ cups green beans, trimmed and cut in 1" pieces

2 cloves garlic, peeled

2 teaspoons dried thyme

Olive oil

Salt and freshly ground pepper to taste

* * * * * *

4 cups chicken stock

1 bay leaf

1. Preheat oven to 400 degrees. Place all the vegetables (carrots through garlic) in a mixing bowl. Toss with thyme, enough olive oil to coat vegetables, salt and pepper. Place vegetables in a single layer on a baking sheet lined with foil. Roast for 45 minutes, turning once or twice, until nicely browned.

2. Transfer vegetables to a large heavy saucepan. Add stock and bay leaf. Bring to a simmer and cook 30–45 minutes. Correct the seasonings and serve.

Serves: 4–6

CHEF'S NOTE

If I find the taste of the soup is not quite right, I'll add a bouillon cube to make the difference.

Roasted vegetables are a great addition to pasta dishes. They can be used as an accompaniment to a meal and are perfect for vegetable lasagna.

SOUTHWEST CORN CHOWDER

6 slices bacon, chopped

2 large onions, chopped

1 stalk celery, chopped

1–1½ teaspoon cumin

¼ cup Pillsbury Unbleached All-Purpose Flour

1 teaspoon salt

4 cups low sodium chicken stock

3 large new potatoes, diced (2–3 cups)

4 ears fresh corn, cut off the cob

1 (15 ounce) can creamed corn

1 cup half and half

8 ounces Pepper Jack cheese, shredded

* * * * * *

Fresh parsley, chopped

1. Cook bacon in a large heavy saucepan over medium heat until crisp. Remove bacon and all but 2 tablespoons bacon grease. Reserve bacon.

2. Add the onions and celery and sauté until onions are translucent. Stir in the cumin, flour, and salt until well absorbed by the bacon fat. Slowly stir in the stock. Add the potatoes and corn. Bring soup to a boil. Reduce the heat to low and simmer covered until the potatoes are softened, about 25 minutes.

3. Over low heat, add the creamed corn, half and half, and cheese; stir until cheese has melted. Remove from heat and correct the seasonings.

4. When ready to serve, garnish with chopped fresh parsley and reserved bacon.

Serves: 8

CHEF'S NOTE

When I cook bacon, I always reserve the grease and store it in a jar in the refrigerator and freeze any leftover bacon. So, as in this case, when a recipe calls for bacon grease and chopped bacon, I already have it and it reduces a cooking step. Take the work out of cooking!

This would be great with Sister Schubert's Buttermilk Biscuits!

TOMATO BASIL SOUP WITH POLENTA

2 tablespoons unsalted butter

1 cup onions, chopped

1 carrot, peeled and diced

2 cloves garlic, chopped

4 cups fresh tomatoes, peeled, seeded and diced or 1 (28 ounce) can diced tomatoes

1 tablespoon tomato paste

1 teaspoon salt

3 cups low sodium chicken stock

2 sprigs of fresh thyme

4 large fresh basil leaves

* * * * * *

1 (14 ounce) can diced tomatoes, drained

2 teaspoons fresh lemon juice

½ cup heavy cream

1. Melt butter over medium heat in large heavy saucepan. Add onions and carrots, sauté to soften, add garlic; sauté a minute more. Add the tomatoes, tomato paste, salt, stock, fresh thyme, and basil. Bring soup to a boil, reduce heat to low, cover and simmer for about 20–25 minutes.

2. While soup is simmering, make the polenta (recipe below).

3. Remove soup from the heat, discard thyme stems. Place soup in a food processor or blender. Puree until smooth. Return to pan and add diced tomatoes, lemon juice and cream to taste. Correct the seasonings.

4. When ready to serve, unmold polenta from ramekins, place in each soup bowl. Pour soup over polenta and garnish with fresh basil.

POLENTA

3 cups milk

1 tablespoon butter

½ teaspoon salt and freshly ground pepper to taste

1 cup cornmeal

¼ cup Miceli's Grated Parmesan Cheese

1. Butter 6–8 ramekins, reserve.

2. Place the milk, butter and seasonings in a heavy saucepan. Bring slowly to a boil. Add the cornmeal gradually while whisking constantly. Reduce heat to low and cook until creamy and thick, once again constantly stirring.

3. Remove from the heat and stir in the Parmesan cheese. Correct the seasonings and pour into prepared ramekins. Polenta can be made the day before and rewarmed for serving.

Serves: 8

 CHEF'S NOTE

A great flavor enhancer for soups is to add a 1" chunk of Parmesan cheese to the soup while it's simmering. It is especially good in this tomato soup and adds a subtle flavor.

Curried Squash and Pear Bisque

2 tablespoons unsalted butter or olive oil

1 butternut squash (about 2¾ pounds), peeled,
    seeds removed and cut into ½" pieces (3½ cups)

1½ cups onion, thinly sliced

2 cups Bartlett pears (about 2 pounds), peeled and cored

2 teaspoons curry powder

½ teaspoon salt

¼ teaspoon black pepper

1 cup pear nectar

4 cups low sodium chicken stock

¼ cup heavy cream

* * * * * *

1 Bartlett pear, cored and thinly sliced

Fresh parsley, chopped

1. Melt butter in a large heavy saucepan over medium heat. Add squash, onions, and pears. Sauté until lightly browned. Add the curry, salt, pepper, pear nectar, and chicken stock. Bring to boil, cover, reduce heat and simmer for 25 minutes.

2. Remove soup to a blender or a food processor and process until smooth. Return soup to pan, add cream, and heat until warm. Correct seasonings.

3. When ready to serve, ladle soup into bowls and garnish with pear slices, and sprinkle with chopped parsley.

Serves: 8

 CHEF'S NOTE

Pear nectar is not difficult to find, look in the juice aisle. If you do have difficulty finding the nectar, you can substitute apple juice.

SPINACH SOUP WITH NUTMEG

1 tablespoon unsalted butter

2 tablespoons shallots, minced

2 tablespoons Pillsbury Unbleached All-Purpose Flour

2 cups low sodium chicken stock

1 cup milk

6 cups spinach, coarsely chopped

2 tablespoons Parmesan cheese

¼ teaspoon fresh nutmeg, grated

1. Melt butter in a medium heavy saucepan over medium heat, add shallots and sauté, but do not brown. Whisk in the flour, stir about a minute to cook the roux. Slowly add the stock to the roux. Whisk to incorporate. Add the milk and chopped spinach. Bring to a slow boil. At this point the soup should be thickened and the spinach cooked. (Do not overcook the spinach; you want those beautiful green leaves.) Correct the seasonings with salt, pepper and nutmeg.

2. When ready to serve, grate some fresh Parmesan cheese in each bowl, and ladle in the soup. Serve immediately.

Serves: 4

CHEF'S NOTE

There are many choices of Parmesan cheese, but, by far, the best flavor comes from Parmigiano Reggiano. It is costly, but it is well worth it.

Photo courtesy of George and Janet Voinovich

One of Nancy Hollister's favorite rooms in the Residence is the kitchen, which she thinks is fabulous.

PARSNIP AND APPLE SOUP TOPPED WITH CRISPY PROSCIUTTO

3 tablespoons unsalted butter, divided

4 cups leeks white and pale green parts, chopped

1 pound parsnips, cut in ½" pieces

2 apples, peeled, cored and cut in ½" pieces

2 cups vegetable or low sodium chicken stock

1½ cups milk

1 teaspoon Dijon mustard

1 tablespoon fresh tarragon, chopped

Salt and freshly ground pepper to taste

½ cup prosciutto, chopped (chopped cooked bacon can be substituted)

1. Melt 2 tablespoons of the butter in a large heavy saucepan over medium heat. Add leeks, parsnips, and apples. Sauté until they just begin to brown. Add the stock; cover and simmer over low heat for about 20 minutes or until the vegetables are softened.

2. In the bowl of a food processor or blender, process the soup in batches. Return the soup back to the saucepan, stir in the milk, mustard, tarragon, salt and pepper. Correct the seasonings and keep warm.

3. When ready to serve, melt the remaining one tablespoon of butter in a small saucepan over medium-high heat. Add prosciutto and sauté until it becomes crispy. Ladle the soup into bowls and top with prosciutto.

Serves: 4–6

CHEF'S NOTE

Parsnips have a pleasantly sweet flavor, which makes them ideal for roasting, grilling, sautéing, and steaming. Also, once boiled they are a lovely addition to mashed potatoes.

GINGERED CARROT SOUP WITH ROASTED PECANS

2 tablespoons unsalted butter

¾ cup onions, chopped

4 cups carrots, sliced thin

2½ tablespoons fresh ginger

¼ teaspoon ground cumin

½ teaspoon salt

3 cups low sodium chicken stock

¼ cup fresh orange juice

* * * * * *

GARNISH

2 tablespoons pecans, chopped

1 teaspoon butter, melted

Dash of salt

¼ cup sour cream

1. Preheat oven to 350 degrees.

2. In a large heavy saucepan, melt butter over moderate heat. Add onion and carrots; cook until onions are translucent. Add ginger, cumin, and salt and cook, stirring, for one minute. Add chicken stock and simmer mixture, covered, 25 minutes, or until carrots are very tender.

3. Prepare pecans while carrot soup is simmering. On a baking sheet, toast pecans in middle of oven 8 minutes, or until fragrant and a shade darker. Toss pecans with butter and salt to taste. Reserve.

4. In a food processor or blender, puree soup until smooth. Stir in the orange juice and correct the seasonings.

5. To serve, ladle soup into bowls, and top with a teaspoonful of sour cream and chopped pecans.

Serves: 6–8

 CHEF'S NOTE

The micro plane zester is a great utensil. It has many uses but, in this recipe, it is very efficient for grating gingerroot. If you don't have one, purchase one; you'll love it.

CHICKEN CURRY SOUP

3 tablespoons unsalted butter

2 cups onions, chopped

2 carrots, peeled and diced

1 tablespoon curry powder, or to taste

¾ teaspoon ground ginger

3 tablespoons flour

5 cups low sodium chicken stock

1 roasted chicken, skin and bones removed, coarsely chopped

¼ cup heavy cream

1 teaspoon fresh lemon juice, or to taste

2 tablespoons fresh parsley, chopped

Salt and freshly ground pepper to taste

GARNISH

Your choice of:

Chopped bacon

Hard cooked eggs

Crosse & Blackwell Capers

Scallions, chopped

1. Melt the butter in a large heavy saucepan, add onions, carrots and cook over low heat until vegetables are tender. Stir in the curry powder, ginger and flour. Cook and stir about 1 minute. Continue to stir while adding the stock. Bring soup to a boil. Reduce heat to low and cover. Simmer about 25 minutes. Add chicken and heat another 5 minutes.

2. Stir in the cream, lemon juice and parsley. Season with salt and pepper. Correct the seasonings and serve hot.

3. Garnish with your choice of chopped bacon, hard cooked eggs, capers and/or scallions.

Serves: 6

CHEF'S NOTE

For a hearty main course, pour soup over cooked rice seasoned with cilantro.

POTAGE SENEGALESE

2 tablespoons unsalted butter

1 onion, minced

1 small apple, peeled and cored, sliced thin

2 teaspoons curry powder, or to taste

4 tablespoons Pillsbury Unbleached All-Purpose Flour

½ cup fresh pea puree or peas baby food

3½ cup low sodium chicken stock

1 cup heavy cream

1. Melt butter in a heavy skillet over medium-low heat. Sauté onions and apples very slowly without browning. Add curry powder and cook slowly another 3 minutes. Stir in flour and pea puree. Stir in chicken stock slowly. Whisk until smooth and until soup comes to a boil. Process soup until smooth and strain through a fine strainer. Push the apples and onions through as much as possible. Add cream and cool.

2. Correct the seasonings. Serve hot or cold.

Serves: 6

CHEF'S NOTE

This is a favorite recipe of Governor Taft's. It comes from his mother and grandmother.

GOVERNOR'S GARDEN GAZPACHO

3 medium fresh tomatoes (about 1½ pounds), cored and diced (4½ cups)

1 green pepper, cored, seeded and diced

1 or 2 cucumbers (12 ounces), peeled, seeded and diced

5 scallions, minced

1 garlic clove, minced

1 teaspoon salt

3 tablespoons sherry wine vinegar

1 tablespoon fresh lemon juice

¼ teaspoon cayenne pepper, or to taste

12 ounces hot and spicy tomato juice

¼ cup fresh parsley, chopped

¼ cup fresh basil, chopped

* * * * * *

GARNISH

T. Marzetti's Restaurant Style Croutons

Sour cream

Fresh arugula

1. Combine tomatoes and their juices, green pepper, cucumbers, scallions, garlic, salt, vinegar, lemon juice and pepper. Allow to stand about 15 minutes so that the vegetables can begin to release their juices. Stir in the tomato juice and fresh herbs. Correct the seasonings and refrigerate for several hours.

2. When ready to serve, garnish gazpacho with a dollop of sour cream, croutons and some chopped fresh arugula. Serve chilled.

Serves: 6–8

CHEF'S NOTE

To create a main course, skewer and grill shrimp basted with pesto sauce. Place the skewered shrimp over the top of the bowl of gazpacho and garnish with a sprig of basil. Serve with a warm loaf of bread.

VICHYSSOISE À LA TAFT

3 tablespoons unsalted butter

2–3 leeks, white part only, sliced (2 cups)

1 medium onion, sliced

1 stalk celery, chopped

5 medium potatoes, thinly sliced

4 cups low sodium chicken stock

1 teaspoon salt

3 cups milk

½–1 cup heavy cream, as desired

* * * * * *

Fresh chives, chopped

1. In a large heavy saucepan, sauté leeks, onions, and celery in butter over medium heat. Do not allow the vegetables to brown. Add the potatoes, chicken stock, and salt. Cover, bring to a boil, reduce the heat and allow to simmer for about 30 minutes or until the potatoes are soft. Puree the soup in a food processor or blender; strain the soup through a fine sieve. Push on the vegetables to push through the flavors. Add the milk and the cream to the strained soup and chill.

2. When ready to serve, correct the seasonings and place soup in serving bowls and garnish with fresh chives.

Serves: 8

CHEF'S NOTE

When you're in a hurry, substitute a good quality prepared potato soup for the potatoes and stock. The soup can be served warm or chilled.

I named this recipe "Vichyssoise à la Taft" because it is one of their favorite summer meals.

DESSERTS & COOKIES

BOB TAFT

GOVERNOR OF OHIO
1999–PRESENT

Bob Taft served his country in the Peace Corps in East Africa and in the Foreign Service in Vietnam. He was a member of the Ohio House of Representatives, a Hamilton County Commissioner and Secretary of State before becoming Governor in 1999. His second term ends in January 2007.

First Lady Hope Taft adopted the giraffe as her mascot because it reminds her to stick her neck out for Ohio's children. She works to keep children drug and alcohol free and visits schools and communities around the state to promote positive youth development. Visitors to the Residence can see her collection of giraffes in the garden room.

HOPE TAFT'S CARROT CAKE

1 cup Crisco Vegetable Oil
2 cups sugar
4 eggs
½ tablespoon vanilla
4 cups carrots, shredded
2 teaspoons baking soda

2 teaspoons salt
2 teaspoons cinnamon
2 cups Pillsbury Unbleached All-
    Purpose Flour
½ cup pecans, toasted and
    chopped (optional)

1. Preheat oven to 350 degrees. Grease 3 (8") round cake pans with Crisco Non-Stick Cooking Spray and line with parchment or wax paper.

2. In the bowl of an electric mixer, add the oil, sugar, eggs, and vanilla. Beat on high speed for about a minute. Beat in the carrots. With the mixer on low speed, add the baking soda, salt and cinnamon. Gradually add in the flour, stir just until the flour is moistened. Fold in the pecans if using. Pour into prepared pans.

3. Bake in preheated oven for 25 minutes or until a toothpick comes out clean. Cool for 5 minutes, remove from pans and cool completely on wire rack.

4. Frost cake with cream cheese frosting, (recipe below). Garnish with chopped pecans around the top edge of cake.

CREAM CHEESE FROSTING

4 tablespoons unsalted butter, softened
2 (3 ounce) packages cream cheese,
    softened

4⅓ cups confectioners' sugar
2 teaspoons vanilla

1. In the bowl of an electric mixer, beat together the butter, cream cheese, and vanilla. Gradually stir in the confectioners' sugar. Beat until smooth and creamy.

Serves 12–15

CHEF'S NOTE

This is Governor Taft's favorite birthday cake. It always comes out perfectly unless you ice it before the cake is completely cooled. You may find that the top layer slides off onto the floor! This information comes from experience according to First Lady Hope Taft.

* * * * * *

Graeter's Cinnamon Ice Cream is a fabulous accompaniment for this cake.

CHOCOLATE TURTLE CAKE

2 ounces unsweetened chocolate,
    melted and cooled

1 cup sugar

¾ cup Pillsbury Unbleached All-
    Purpose Flour

½ teaspoon baking soda

¼ teaspoon salt

½ cup strong brewed coffee

¼ cup sour cream

¼ cup Crisco Vegetable Oil

1 teaspoon vanilla

1 egg

* * * * * *

¾ cup heavy cream

6 ounces semi-sweet chocolate

* * * * * *

½ cup pecans, toasted and chopped

Robert Rothschild Old Fashion
    Caramel Sauce

1. Preheat oven to 350 degrees. Lightly grease with Crisco Non-Stick Cooking Spray one 8" round cake pan. Line pan with either parchment paper or waxed paper.

2. In an electric mixing bowl fitted with the whisk attachment, add the sugar, flour, baking soda, and salt. Turn the mixer on low speed to combine.

3. Mix the coffee, sour cream, oil, and vanilla together and slowly add to the flour mixture. Mix until well combined, scraping the sides of the bowl several times.

4. Add the egg and beat for about 30 seconds. Stir in the chocolate and pour batter into prepared pan. Place cake in the preheated oven and bake for about 30–35 minutes or until a toothpick comes out clean. Remove cake from pan and place on cooling rack after 10 minutes. Cool completely.

5. For the ganache, place chocolate in a stainless steel bowl, heat cream to boiling and pour cream mixture over chocolate. Allow mixture to stand for about 5 minutes. Stir until smooth. Cool to room temperature.

6. To assemble cake; Make sure your ganache is at room temperature and just a bit fluid. The frosting needs to drizzle down the edges of the cake. Slice cake in 2 equal halves, horizontally. Place the bottom layer on a cake plate. Spread with some of the ganache, top with ¼ cup of the pecans and place top layer over bottom. Spread the ganache on the top of the cake, allowing the chocolate to drip down the edges of the cake. Sprinkle the remaining ¼ cup pecans over the top of the cake. Drizzle caramel sauce generously over top of the pecans.

Serves: 12

CHEF'S NOTE

If you want a great chocolate layer cake, double the cake and the ganache ingredients.

This chocolate layer cake is getting a reputation as Governor Taft's "famous chocolate cake".

CHOCOLATE BLACK RASPBERRY CHIP
ICE CREAM CAKE ROLL

3 eggs

1 cup sugar

⅓ cup water

1 teaspoon vanilla

1 cup cake flour

¼ cup unsweetened cocoa powder

1 teaspoon baking powder

¼ teaspoon salt

* * * * * *

1 quart Graeter's Black Raspberry Chip Ice Cream, slightly softened

Powdered sugar

Whipped cream

1. Heat oven to 375 degrees. Line a jelly roll pan with aluminum foil and grease generously.

2. Beat eggs and sugar in a large mixing bowl until very thick and lemon colored, about 3 minutes. Carefully fold in the water and vanilla.

3. Place cake flour, cocoa powder, baking powder, and salt in a sifter and sift to combine. Slowly fold into batter. Fold until batter is smooth. Pour evenly into prepared pan and bake for 12 to 15 minutes (don't spread batter with spatula as you will lose some of the air in the batter).

4. Generously sprinkle a clean kitchen towel with powdered sugar. When cake is finished baking, immediately invert pan over sugared towel. Carefully and quickly remove the foil from the cake. While hot, roll cake in the towel from the long end. Cool cake on a wire rack for at least 30 minutes. Very carefully unroll cake, place ½" slices of ice cream on the cake, leaving the edges exposed. Carefully roll up cake tightly, releasing the cake from the towel. Wrap tightly in plastic wrap and freeze until ready to serve.

5. When ready to serve, dust cake with powdered sugar. Slice a 1" piece of cake roll onto the plate, top with whipped cream and enjoy.

Serves: 12

CHEF'S NOTE

This is a sponge cake. Its primary leavening comes from the air beaten into it. So be careful not to over mix when folding the dry ingredients into the batter.

FLOURLESS CHOCOLATE CAKE

12 ounces semisweet chocolate,
   broken in small chunks
¾ cup unsalted butter, cut in chunks
2 tablespoons instant coffee granules
¼ cup cocoa powder
5 eggs

⅔ cup sugar
½ tablespoon vanilla
* * * * * *
Confectioners' sugar
Whipped cream

1. Preheat oven to 325 degrees. Generously butter a 9" springform pan.

2. Place the chocolate, butter, and coffee granules in top of a double boiler over simmering water. Cook, stirring constantly, until chocolate has melted. Stir in cocoa powder until the mixture is smooth. Remove from heat and set aside to cool.

3. In the bowl of an electric mixer fitted with the whisk attachment, beat the eggs, sugar, and vanilla. Whisk until the mixture has doubled in volume and is pale in color, about 2–3 minutes.

4. Pour in the cooled chocolate. Slowly increase speed to medium-high and beat for a few seconds or until batter is well blended.

5. Pour into the prepared pan and bake in the preheated oven for 40–50 minutes or until the center is no longer loose. Remove from the oven and cool on a rack. Run a knife around the edge of the pan to loosen cake. Cover cake and refrigerate until cold.

6. Before serving, remove cake from the pan onto a serving plate. Sprinkle cake with confectioners' sugar or pipe rosettes of whipped cream around the edge of the cake. Serve with Crème Anglaise.

CRÈME ANGLAISE

1 cup heavy cream, heated
1 cup milk, heated
5 egg yolks

½ cup sugar
2 teaspoons vanilla

1. Combine cream, milk, egg yolks, and sugar in the top of a double boiler over simmering water. Cook, stirring frequently until the sauce thickens and coats the back of a spoon or a thermometer reaches 160 degrees. Remove from heat and stir in vanilla. Chill thoroughly before serving. To store, place a piece of plastic wrap to fit snugly on top of the sauce. Cover tightly and refrigerate until needed.

Serves: 12

CHEF'S NOTE

Eggs coagulate and begin to thicken at 160 degrees. I use a thermometer when making Crème Anglaise to make sure that thickening begins and the eggs do not coagulate (or you'll have scrambled eggs!).

FARMHOUSE RASPBERRY SHORTCAKE

1 quart fresh raspberries

Robert Rothschild Red Raspberry Gourmet Sauce

* * * * * *

2 cups Pillsbury Unbleached All-Purpose Flour, sifted

2 tablespoons sugar

1 teaspoon salt

4 teaspoons baking powder

6 tablespoons unsalted butter, cold and cut in pieces

¾–1 cup milk

2 tablespoons butter

* * * * * *

1¾ cup heavy cream, divided

Fresh mint for garnish

1. Preheat oven to 450 degrees.

2. Mix together the bottle of red raspberry sauce and fresh raspberries. Reserve.

3. In a mixing bowl, combine the sifted flour, sugar, salt, and baking powder. Using a pastry blender, cut in 6 tablespoons butter until the mixture looks like meal. Stir in the milk; use just enough to make a soft dough. Place dough on a lightly floured board and knead lightly about 10 times. Place dough in an 8" ungreased round cake pan and pat dough lightly in place. Dot with the remaining 2 tablespoons butter and sprinkle with sugar.

4. Bake in preheated oven for 12–15 minutes. Remove cake from pan and place on cooling rack and cool to warm.

5. In a large mixing bowl, beat 1 cup of cream until it almost reaches the butter stage. Cut shortcake in half, horizontally. Spread each inside half with whipped butter. Place half the red raspberries on the bottom layer of shortcake. Replace the top buttered layer on the raspberries and cover with the remaining berries. Whip the remaining 1 cup cream to soft peaks. Serve the shortcake with a dollop of whipped cream and fresh mint.

Serves: 8

 CHEF'S NOTE

I use raw sugar to sprinkle on pie crusts, scones, and biscuits before they are baked. The sugar doesn't dissolve completely therefore making a pretty presentation.

MOLTEN CHOCOLATE CAKE

½ cup unsalted butter

4 ounces good quality semi-sweet chocolate, finely chopped

2 ounces unsweetened chocolate, finely chopped

2 tablespoons unsweetened cocoa powder

1 tablespoon instant coffee

⅓ sugar

¾ cup brown sugar

3 eggs

¾ teaspoon baking powder

⅓ cup Pillsbury Unbleached All-Purpose Flour

* * * * * *

Graeter's Vanilla Ice Cream

Cocoa powder

1. Generously butter 6–8 ramekins with butter and set aside.

2. Melt the butter in a heavy medium saucepan over low heat. Add the semi-sweet and unsweetened chocolate, stir until almost melted. Stir in the cocoa powder, instant coffee and both sugars. Stir until the chocolate is melted and sugar and coffee granules are fully dissolved.

3. Remove from the heat and pour into bowl of an electric mixer. With mixer on low speed, add the eggs one at a time, the baking powder, and flour. Increase speed to medium-high and beat for 5 minutes.

4. Place mixture in prepared ramekins, filling about half full. Cover with plastic wrap and freeze for at least 3 hours.

5. When ready to serve, preheat oven to 375 degrees.

6. Place ramekins on a baking sheet, then in the oven on the middle rack. Bake until edges are set but centers are still shiny, about 10 to 15 minutes. Do not overcook; if unsure reserve one ramekin as a tester. Serve immediately.

7. Invert onto a serving dish and serve with ice cream. Garnish with a dusting of cocoa powder.

Serves: 6–8

 CHEF'S NOTE

This may be the best of the best. It's easy to prepare, the flavor is amazing and it must be made ahead of time. In fact, if you don't use all eight, keep them in the freezer for use at another time.

GOVERNOR'S APPLE CAKE

1 cup Pillsbury Unbleached All-Purpose Flour

1 teaspoon baking soda

1 teaspoon cinnamon

½ teaspoon allspice

¼ teaspoon nutmeg

¼ teaspoon salt

¾ cup sugar

⅓ cup unsalted butter, melted

1 egg

2 cups apples, peeled and chopped ½" or 1½ cup apples and ½ cup pears

½ cup walnuts, toasted and chopped

* * * * * *

Confectioners' sugar

Robert Rothschild Cinnamon Bun Caramel Dessert Sauce, warmed

1. Preheat oven to 350 degrees. Grease an 8" cake pan with Crisco Non-Stick Cooking Spray.

2. In a mixing bowl, combine the flour, baking soda, spices, and salt. In another bowl, mix the sugar, melted butter, egg, apples, and walnuts. Add the dry ingredients to the apple mixture; stir to combine. Transfer the batter to the prepared pan.

3. Place in preheated oven and bake about 40–45 minutes or until tester comes out clean.

4. Dust with confectioners' sugar. Serve warm with cinnamon bun caramel sauce.

Serves: 8

CHEF'S NOTE

This cake is truly a comfort food. It is quick and easy to prepare and it will stay moist and fresh for several days.

This cake has been a favorite of all three Governors I've served.

DOUBLE CHOCOLATE BREAD PUDDING

8 cups brioche or egg buns, cut in ½" cubes

2¾ cups milk

⅓ cup sugar

⅓ cup unsweetened cocoa

¼ cup strong coffee

1 tablespoon vanilla

4 eggs

2 egg yolks

* * * * * *

1 cup chocolate chunks

Graeter's Vanilla Ice Cream

CHEF'S NOTE

The beauty of this bread pudding is that it can be sliced. The presentation is unique and the flavor is rich and luscious.

This dish needs to be cooked in a water bath. The technique is designed to cook delicate dishes such as custards and sauces without curdling them. It's also a great way to keep foods warm.

1. Preheat oven to 350 degrees. Butter a 9" springform pan.

2. Spread bread cubes in a single layer on a baking sheet. Bake about 10–15 minutes to toast bread. Reduce oven to 325 degrees.

3. In a mixing bowl, whisk together the milk, sugar, cocoa, coffee, vanilla, eggs, and egg yolks until thoroughly mixed. Fold in bread cubes carefully to coat, cover, and refrigerate at least 30 minutes or more.

4. Pour bread custard into prepared pan; sprinkle chocolate chunks evenly over the top. Place baking dish in a larger baking dish than itself to create a water bath. Pour simmering water in larger pan so it reaches 1" up the sides of the pan. Carefully place in preheated oven and bake 40 minutes or until pudding is set. Allow pudding to cool at room temperature about 30 minutes. Slice each piece and place on serving plate, serve warm with vanilla ice cream.

Serves: 9–12

Both Governor and Mrs. Taft are volunteers for Ohio Reads, a program started by Governor Taft that brings 50,000 volunteers into elementary schools to help children become good readers.

Pumpkin Crème Caramel with Maple Cream

1 cup sugar

⅓ cup water

* * * * * *

1 cup whole milk

¾ cup heavy cream, divided

1 (15 ounce) can pure pumpkin

2 teaspoons pumpkin pie spice

4 egg yolks plus 2 eggs

1 cup sugar

1 teaspoon vanilla

* * * * * *

3 tablespoons pure Ohio maple syrup

1 cup heavy cream

1. Preheat oven to 325 degrees.

2. Place sugar and water in a medium heavy saucepan over medium-high heat. Stir just to dissolve the sugar. Continue to cook without stirring. When the mixture has caramelized and turned a rich amber brown, divide among 8 (1 cup) custard cups. Swirl each cup to distribute caramel. Reserve.

3. Combine the milk, ¾ cup cream, pumpkin and pumpkin pie spice in a medium heavy saucepan over medium heat. Stir and warm mixture just to a simmer.

4. Place the eggs and egg yolks in the bowl of an electric mixer. Beat on low speed to mix, gradually add the sugar and vanilla. Add the pumpkin/cream mixture slowly to the eggs and sugar. Divide the custard among the 8 custard cups. Place cups in a large pan filled with simmering water bath. The hot water should be half way up the sides of the custard cups. Place in preheated oven. Bake for about 50 minutes. Custard should be slightly soft in the center. Remove from water bath and refrigerate, uncovered until cold.

5. When ready to serve, beat remaining 1 cup cream with maple syrup until it reaches soft peaks. Invert pumpkin custard onto a serving plate and top with maple cream.

Serves: 8

CHEF'S NOTE

When making the caramel, there are two very important points. One, DO NOT STIR the mixture once the sugar and water are combined. Additional stirring will cause the caramel to crystallize. Two, as soon as the caramel begins to brown, don't walk away. There is a point when the caramel is amber brown and perfect, then quickly it can burn and become unusable.

COFFEE CHIP BAKED ALASKA

1 purchased Pillsbury Fudge
   Brownie Mix

* * * * * *

½ cup heavy cream

4 ounces semisweet chocolate chips

* * * * * *

1 pint Graeter's Mocha Chip, softened

3 tablespoons strong coffee

* * * * * *

4 egg whites, room temperature

¼ teaspoon cream of tartar

Pinch of salt

⅔ cup sugar

½ teaspoon vanilla

1. Prepare brownie mix according to package directions; allow to cool. Cut 6 rounds which match the size of your muffin tin openings.

2. Heat heavy cream to a boil; remove from heat and add the chocolate chips. Allow to sit for a few minutes. Whisk to combine. Cool and reserve.

3. Line a 6 cup muffin tin with paper cups. Press ½ cup of the ice cream into each prepared cup, leaving a ½" space on top for the brownie. Spoon 1 tablespoon cooled chocolate sauce over the ice cream. Place brownie round in each muffin cup. Drizzle 2 teaspoons of coffee over each of the 6 rounds. Cover pan thoroughly with plastic wrap and freeze overnight.

4. Preheat oven to 500 degrees.

5. In the bowl of a large clean mixing bowl, add the egg whites, cream of tartar and salt. Beat on medium high until foam holds a soft peak.

6. Sprinkle in the sugar 1 tablespoon at a time. Give the foam some time to dissolve the sugar, about 10–15 seconds between each addition. When the meringue is very stiff and shiny, add in the vanilla.

7. Remove the paper from the ice cream. Place the Alaska brownie side down on a very cold parchment lined baking sheet. Generously cover each Alaska with meringue. Be sure meringue reaches the parchment paper to encase the ice cream.

8. Bake in preheated oven on the top third rack for 4–5 minutes. The meringue tips should be nicely darkened. Serve immediately on chilled plates.

CHEF'S NOTE

For best results, begin this dessert the day before serving.

Be aware that any fat (egg yolks) that get into the whites will prevent the egg whites from reaching their full volume.

I have found that once I apply the meringue, they can stay in the freezer for about 10–15 minutes before they go in the oven.

Serves: 6

RICE PUDDING CRÈME BRÛLÉE

⅓ cup short-grain rice such as Arborio

4 cups milk

1 cinnamon stick

⅓ cup sugar

¼ cup raisins

½ tablespoon vanilla

½ teaspoon freshly grated nutmeg

* * * * * *

½ cup pure cane raw sugar

CHEF'S NOTE

I have tried a variety of sugars for Crème Brûlée and have found the raw sugar definitely works best.

Use a kitchen torch to caramelize Crème Brûlée. To use the torch, move the flame continuously in small circles around the surface until the sugar melts, bubbles and lightly browns.

1. Preheat oven to 300 degrees.

2. In a heavy saucepan, add the rice, milk, and cinnamon stick. Cover and bring to a simmer over medium heat. Reduce heat to low, simmer gently. Stir occasionally, until rice is very tender, about 30 minutes. Remove from heat, stir in the sugar, raisins, vanilla, and nutmeg. Pour the rice pudding into a buttered baking dish and bake for 1 hour. Remove cinnamon stick. Pudding will be creamy. Chill.

3. Just before serving, preheat broiler and blot the top of the custard dry with a paper towel. Sprinkle raw sugar evenly over the pudding. Place pudding in a dish of ice water and broil custard about 2" from the heat source. Heat until the sugar is melted and crisp. Be careful not to burn the sugar.

Serves: 6–8

Governor Taft continues a family tradition of planting a live Christmas tree at the end of the holiday season. Several of the evergreen trees around the property are Christmas trees from years he has been in office.

Ice Cream Buckeye with Ohio Chocolate Mousse Cake

Ice cream Buckeye

1 quart Graeter's Peanut Butter Ice Cream
Smucker's Chocolate Magic Shell Ice Cream Topping

* * * * * *

Ohio Chocolate Mousse

¾ cup water

¼ cup sugar

½ cup butter, cut into pieces

18 ounces semisweet chocolate, broken into small pieces

7 eggs

2 tablespoons strong coffee

* * * * * *

Garnish

Fresh buckeye leaf, cleaned and patted dry
Robert Rothschild Red Raspberry Gourmet Sauce

1. Scoop out at least 12 round balls with a 1½" ice cream scoop; place on a very cold jelly roll pan. Place the rough looking balls in the freezer; and allow to set. Remove from freezer and with your hands, roll ice cream into more of a round ball. Return to freezer and freeze overnight.

2. Pour magic shell chocolate into a 2"–3" cup. Dip frozen ice cream into chocolate, leaving a nickel-size opening of ice cream. The ice cream ball should resemble a buckeye. Gently wipe off the bottom of your ice cream buckeye on the side of the cup so the chocolate won't spread on the cold baking sheet. Repeat with the remaining balls of ice cream, freeze until ready to use.

3. Preheat oven to 350 degrees. Line a jelly roll pan with parchment paper or aluminum foil. Lightly spray with Crisco Non-Stick Cooking Spray.

4. In a medium heavy saucepan, bring water and sugar to a simmer over medium heat. Stir to dissolve the sugar. Add butter and stir until butter is melted. Remove pan from the heat and add in the chocolate. Swirl the pan to distribute, allow to stand until chocolate is melted.

5. In a mixing bowl, whisk together the eggs and coffee until just combined.

6. Whisk chocolate until smooth, and then whisk the chocolate into the egg mixture. Pour into prepared pan. If you have a larger pan than a jelly roll pan, it is best to bake the mousse in a water bath. Bake for 40 minutes or until mousse is firm in the center. Allow to set about 10 minutes. With an Ohio cookie cutter, cut out your Ohio shapes. Remove scraps and leave shapes in the pan, wrap in plastic wrap and refrigerate.

7. Place the raspberry sauce in a blender and process until smooth. The red raspberry gourmet sauce makes a quick and tasty coulis.

8. When ready to serve, place a pool of raspberry sauce on a serving plate. To the edge of the sauce, place the Ohio mousse and the frozen buckeye. Add the buckeye leaf and enjoy the reaction you will get from your guests.

Serves: 12

CHEF'S NOTE

This has been the perfect dessert to serve when we've entertained Governors and representatives from other states. We gleam with pride.

Dinner

Saganaki with Fresh Tuna Nicoise

Filet with Duxelle Puff Pastry topped with a Stilton Herbed Ravioli
Herbed Scented Baby Squash with Petit Haricots

Angel Light Double Raspberry Gateau with Chocolate Lattice

The Ohio Governor's Residence
Thursday, August 19, 1999

When Governor Bush was finished with his meal he came into the kitchen and commented, "somebody back here sure knows how to cook a steak." To which June McCarthy replied, "That would be me!"

Mixed Berry Summer Pudding

1 loaf Pepperidge Farm Toasting White Bread, crusts removed

2 cups red raspberries

2 cups blueberries

2 cups strawberries, sliced

¾ cup sugar

1 teaspoon powdered gelatin

1 teaspoon sugar

2 tablespoons warm water

* * * * * *

1 cup heavy cream

2 tablespoons confectioners' sugar

1. Spray a 6-cup pâté pan or 8"x4" loaf pan with Crisco Non-Stick Cooking Spray. Line the pan with plastic wrap or aluminum foil.

2. Line the pan, on the bottom and around, with one layer of bread slices.

3. In a large saucepan, over medium heat, add the fruits and sugar. Gently stir to combine. Cook the fruit until it is just tender, about 5 minutes. Remove from heat and cool slightly. Combine gelatin with 1 teaspoon sugar, dissolve the gelatin/sugar in the warm water and fold into the berries. Place the fruit in the bread-lined pan.

4. Top the fruit with another layer of bread so the fruit is completely covered. Wrap the whole pan with double the layers of plastic wrap. Place a weight over the plastic wrap (like heavy cans). Refrigerate at least 6 hours or overnight.

5. When ready to serve, whip the heavy cream in a cold bowl with the confectioners' sugar until it reaches soft peaks. Remove weights and plastic wrap from pan. Place a large serving plate over the pan and invert. Serve with whipped cream. Garnish with extra berries and sprig of fresh mint.

Serves: 8

Chef's Note

Avoid dissolving gelatin in hot water. Hot water may cause the gelatin granules to lump together. To make sure this doesn't happen, mix together gelatin with some sugar to separate the granules and then dissolve in warm, not hot, water.

CHOCOLATE SWIRL CUPCAKES

FILLING

1 cup Miceli's Whole Milk Ricotta

¼ cup sugar

1 egg

1 teaspoon vanilla

⅛ teaspoon salt

1 cup miniature semi-sweet
    chocolate chips, divided

CUPCAKE

⅓ cup Crisco Vegetable Oil

1 cup sugar

1 egg

1 tablespoon vanilla

½ teaspoon salt

1 teaspoon baking soda

½ cup milk

⅓ cup cocoa powder

1½ cups Pillsbury All-Purpose Flour

1. Combine all filling ingredients, except use only ½ cup of the chocolate chips. Place in the refrigerator to chill.

2. Preheat oven to 350 degrees. Spray non-stick muffin tin with Crisco Non-Stick Cooking Spray.

3. In the bowl of an electric mixer, beat together the oil and sugar. Add the egg and vanilla, beat well. With the mixer on slow speed, stir in the salt and baking soda. Stir in half the milk, the cocoa powder, the other half of the milk and finally the flour. Mix to combine.

4. Place in each muffin cup 2 tablespoons of cake batter, top with 1 tablespoon ricotta batter and a few chocolate chips. Swirl with a knife to create a marbled batter.

5. Bake in preheated oven for 25–30 minutes.

Serves: 15

 CHEF'S NOTE

This recipe is lots of fun to make with the kids. There is nothing more special than cooking with your children.

BUTTER PASTRY

2 eggs

1 tablespoon white vinegar

Crushed ice

12 ounces (2½ cups) Pillsbury
    Unbleached All-Purpose Flour

1 tablespoon sugar

½ teaspoon salt

1 cup butter, cold, cut in chunks

CHEF'S NOTE

*Sugar used in a pastry dough helps
to brown and tenderize the crust.*

*The vinegar also helps to tenderize
the pastry.*

1. In a small bowl beat together the egg, vinegar, and crushed ice. Reserve.

2. In a large mixing bowl, combine the flour, sugar, and salt. Using a pastry blender, cut in the cold butter until the mixture is crumbly and the butter is the size of large peas. It's the pockets of fat that creates a flaky crust.

3. Sprinkle about ¼ cup egg/vinegar blend around the flour. With a rubber spatula, work enough water into the flour just until large clumps are formed. Use the broad side of a spatula, pressing down on the dough to create the clumps of dough (It should not come together in a ball.) Transfer dough onto a clean surface. Push together dough to form 2 discs. Wrap in plastic wrap and refrigerate at least 30 minutes. Refrigerating several hours is better as it relaxes the gluten in the dough.

4. Roll chilled dough on a lightly floured surface to a 12" round, ¼" thick. Mold dough in a 9" pie pan or as directed by the recipe.

Yields: 2 (9") Pastry Crusts

Photo by Claudia Retter, Alon Arts

*One of the Tafts' favorite annual events
is the reception for Ohio artisans who
create ornaments for the Residence
Christmas Tree through the
Treasures for the Tree Contest.*

GRAETER'S PEANUT BUTTER AND BANANA CHOCOLATE ICE CREAM PIE

4 ounces semi-sweet chocolate

½ cup heavy cream

PEANUT BUTTER CRUST

1¼ cups graham cracker crumbs

¼ cup honey

⅓ cup Jif Creamy Peanut Butter

* * * * * *

¼ cup honey

3 cups mashed ripe bananas (about 4 bananas)

½ teaspoon fresh lemon juice

1 pint Graeter's Buckeye Blitz ice cream, softened

1. To make the topping, place the semi-sweet chocolate in a bowl. Heat the heavy cream to boiling, and pour over the chocolate and allow the chocolate to melt. Stir until completely combined. Cool to room temperature.

2. In the bowl of an electric mixer fitted with the beater bar, combine cracker crumbs, ¼ cup honey and peanut butter. Press crust into bottom and up the sides of a 9" pie pan.

3. Combine honey, bananas, and lemon juice in a large heavy skillet over medium heat. Cook until mixture thickens, about 5 minutes, stirring frequently. Cool completely.

4. Wipe out mixing bowl and add softened ice cream; beat on medium speed until smooth. Fold in banana mixture. Spoon into crust and smooth top. Freeze until firm.

5. Drizzle chocolate back and forth on top of frozen pie. Chill the chocolate until it is firm enough to pipe. Place the remaining chocolate in a pastry bag fitted with a star tip. Pipe rosettes around the edge of the pie. Freeze until ready to serve. Allow pie to soften in the refrigerator for 30 minutes before cutting and serving.

Serves: 8

CHEF'S NOTE

The topping for this dessert is actually a ganache, which is a rich chocolate icing. Ganache is cooled to room temperature and used to glaze cakes, pastries, and tortes.

MACAROON LEMON PIE

1 (9") pastry shell *(see page 136)*

FILLING

3 eggs

2 egg yolks

¼ teaspoon salt

1¼ cups sugar

1 cup shredded sweetened coconut

1 cup heavy cream, divided

¼ cup fresh lemon juice

2 tablespoons unsalted butter, melted

2 teaspoons lemon zest

2½ teaspoons vanilla, divided

½ teaspoon coconut extract

1 tablespoon confectioners' sugar

* * * * * *

8 thin lemon slices

1. Preheat oven to 350 degrees.

2. Roll pastry to fit a 9" pie shell. Trim crust leaving a ½" overhang. Fold edge under and crimp decoratively. Line crust with foil and fill pastry with dried beans or pie weights. Bake until crust is set and slightly browned, about 20 minutes. Remove foil and beans. Cool slightly

3. In the bowl of an electric mixer, beat together the eggs, egg yolks, and salt. Add in the sugar and beat until mixture is thick and fluffy, about 1 minute. Stir in coconut, ¼ cup heavy cream, lemon juice, melted butter, lemon zest, 1½ teaspoons vanilla, and coconut extract.

4. Pour filling into precooked pastry. Bake until filling is set and knife inserted comes out clean, about 40 minutes. Remove to a cooling rack and refrigerate until well chilled.

5. Place remaining ¾ cup cream, confectioners' sugar, and remaining 1 teaspoon vanilla in a large bowl. Beat until stiff peaks form. Pipe whipped cream around the edge of the pie and garnish with lemon slices.

Serves 8–12

CHEF'S NOTE

All recipes are based on the use of large eggs.

This recipe is a favorite of the Governor's Residence housekeeper, Mona Reed, who has lovingly taken care of the Residence since 1987.

CHERRY-RASPBERRY LATTICE PIE

Pastry for Double-Crust Pie *(see page 136)*

* * * * * *

1¼ cups sugar

½ cup Pillsbury Unbleached All-Purpose Flour

2 cups fresh or frozen red raspberries

2 cups fresh or frozen unsweetened pitted tart red cherries

½ teaspoon almond extract

1. Prepare and roll out pastry as directed.

2. Preheat oven to 450 degrees. Line a 9" pie plate with half of the pastry. Trim pastry ½" from the edge of the pie plate.

3. In a large mixing bowl combine sugar and flour. Add raspberries, cherries, and almond extract. Toss gently until fruit is coated. Stir filling; transfer to pastry-lined pie plate.

4. Roll pastry to a 12" circle. Cut circle into strips ½"–1" wide. Place 5–7 strips across the filling in the pie pan. Starting at one edge, weave one strip at a time over and under each crosswise strip, equidistant apart. Tuck, seal, and crimp edge of pastry. Brush lightly with milk to help brown crust and sprinkle with sugar. Bake in preheated 450 degree oven for 15 minutes. Reduce heat to 350 degrees and continue to bake another 45 minutes or until filling is bubbly and crust is golden. Cool on a rack.

Serves: 8

CHEF'S NOTE

To be sure pies are thickened properly, make sure pie filling is bubbling in the center as well as around the edges.

THE RESIDENCE CHOCOLATE CHUNK COOKIES

1 cup unsalted butter, softened

2 tablespoons light corn syrup

1 cup brown sugar

½ cup sugar

1 egg

1 egg yolk

1 tablespoon vanilla

¾ teaspoon baking soda

¾ teaspoon salt

14 ounces Pillsbury Unbleached All-Purpose Flour

3 cups chocolate chunks or 2 cups chocolate chunks and 1 cup pecans, toasted
and chopped

1. Preheat oven to 375 degrees. Place parchment paper on baking sheets.

2. In the bowl of an electric mixer, beat together the butter, corn syrup, brown sugar and
    sugar until well creamed. Beat in the eggs one at a time and add vanilla. With the
    mixer on low speed, stir in the baking soda and salt. Gradually add the flour until
    incorporated. Stir in the chocolate chunks.

3. Using a small ice cream scoop or spoon, drop cookies on prepared baking sheet about
    2" apart. Bake in a preheated oven for about 10–12 minutes or until cookies are light-
    ly browned. Do not overbake. Remove to a cooling rack and enjoy!

For Thin and Crispy Cookies:
Increase corn syrup to ¼ cup,
eliminate egg yolk, and reduce
the flour to 13 ounces.

Yield: 3 dozen

CHEF'S NOTE

*I have found that weighing the
flour gives a more consistent
cookie. FYI, 14 ounces equals
approximately 2¾ cup flour.*

Mrs. Taft teaches children about plants of Ohio
in the Residence gardens.

PEANUT BUTTER OATMEAL CHIP COOKIES

¾ cup unsalted butter, softened

1 cup sugar

1 cup brown sugar

1¾ cups Jif Extra Crunchy Peanut Butter

4 eggs

½ tablespoon vanilla

½ teaspoon salt

2½ teaspoons baking soda

4 cups oatmeal

¾ cup Pillsbury Unbleached All-Purpose Flour

12 ounces chocolate chips

10 ounces peanut butter chips

CHEF'S NOTE

Shiny heavy gauge aluminum cookie sheets will produce evenly baked and properly browned cookies. Remember shiny surfaces reflect heat while dark surfaces absorb heat and tend to over-brown cookies.

1. Preheat the oven to 350 degrees. Line baking sheets with parchment paper.

2. In a large mixing bowl, beat together the butter, sugars, and peanut butter. When thoroughly combined, add the eggs, one at a time, beating after each addition. With the mixer on low, add the vanilla, salt, and soda. Add in the oatmeal and flour. Stir in the chocolate chips and peanut butter chips.

3. Bake about 10 minutes or until the cookies begin to brown on the bottom. Do not over bake.

Yield: 4 dozen

The Tafts established the Ohio Heritage Garden that replicates the diverse growing regions of the state. They have also installed a solar panel array on the roof of the carriage house to provide emergency power.

Snickerdoodles

1 cup unsalted butter, softened

1½ cups sugar

3 eggs

1 tablespoon vanilla

½ teaspoon nutmeg

½ tablespoon cinnamon

½ teaspoon cream of tartar

½ teaspoon salt

1 teaspoon baking soda

3¼ cup Pillsbury Unbleached All-Purpose Flour

* * * * * *

¼ cup sugar

2 teaspoons cinnamon

1. Preheat oven to 350 degrees. Line baking sheets with parchment paper.

2. In the bowl of an electric mixer fitted with the beater bar, add the butter and sugar and beat until creamy. Add in the eggs and egg yolks, one at a time, beating well to incorporate. With the mixer on low speed, add in the vanilla, nutmeg, cream of tartar, salt and baking soda. Slowly add in the flour and mix to combine. In a small bowl, stir together the sugar and cinnamon. Reserve.

3. With a number 40 ice cream scoop, place balls of dough on baking sheet spacing 2" apart. Chill cookies for about 15 minutes. When cookies are chilled and firm, form into balls, then roll in cinnamon/sugar.

4. Bake in preheated oven for 10 minutes, or until lightly brown. Allow cookies to set and then remove to a cooling rack.

Yields: 4 dozen

Chef's Note

> *Nutmeg is a wonderful spice. It is especially flavorful when it is freshly grated from whole nutmeg. It is a must in my kitchen!*

CHOCOLATE WALNUT BROWNIES

1 cup sugar

4 tablespoons unsalted butter

¼ cup water

3¾ cups semi-sweet chocolate chips

3 eggs slightly beaten

1 tablespoon vanilla

1¼ cup Pillsbury Unbleached All-Purpose Flour

½ teaspoon baking soda

½ teaspoon salt

¾ cup walnuts, chopped and toasted (optional)

CHEF'S NOTE

To test the doneness for brownies, place your toothpick closer to the edges and not in the center. This keeps the brownies moist.

1. Preheat oven to 325 degrees. Spray a 9"x13" baking pan with Crisco Non-Stick Cooking Spray.

2. Cut butter into 2" sections. Melt butter, sugar, and water in a medium saucepan over low heat; stir until mixture boils. Remove from heat. Immediately stir in 2 cups of chips, stirring until melted. Cool slightly.

3. Stir in eggs and vanilla until blended. Finally add in the baking soda, salt, and flour into the chocolate mixture. Cool slightly. Stir in 1 cup chocolate chips and the walnuts.

4. Pour into prepared pan. Sprinkle the remaining ¾ cup chips over the top. Bake at 350 degrees for 25 to 30 minutes. Cool completely before cutting.

Yields: 24 bars

Governor Taft assists Chef June McCarthy with a cooking demonstration at the Ohio State Fair.

Photo by Chris Kasson, Office of the Governor

INDEX

INDEX